YO

GENERAL EDITOR
Professor A.N. Jeffares
(*University of Stirling*)

STUDYING THOMAS HARDY

Lance St John Butler

MA (CAMBRIDGE) PH D (STIRLING)
*Lecturer in English Studies,
University of Stirling*

YORK PRESS
Immeuble Esseily, Place Riad Solh, Beirut.

LONGMAN GROUP UK LIMITED
Longman House,
Burnt Mill,
Harlow,
Essex

First published 1986
Reprinted 1989

ISBN 0-582-79285-1

Produced by Longman Group (FE) Ltd
Printed in Hong Kong

Contents

PLATES

Chapter 1

Hardy's life and times

Studying Hardy

We can learn about Hardy himself, 'Hardy the man', in three ways. First there are the biographies of him: immediately after his death his second wife completed and published a two-volume biography which, it is clear, was in large part written or dictated by Hardy himself (F.E. Hardy, *The Life of Thomas Hardy*, first one-volume edn, Macmillan, London, 1962) and in more recent years there have been two excellent biographies, one by Robert Gittings (*Young Thomas Hardy*, Heinemann Educational, London, 1975, and *The Older Hardy*, Heinemann Educational, London, 1978) and one by Michael Millgate (*Thomas Hardy: A Biography*, Oxford University Press, Oxford, 1982). In addition there is a good illustrated biography by Timothy O'Sullivan (Macmillan, London, 1975).

Second, there are Hardy's poems. Hardy was an exceptionally personal poet. He experimented with all sorts of disguises but in the end, and in his greatest poems, he spoke directly of the personal details and emotions of his own life in a way that has only become common among more modern poets.

Third, there are Hardy's novels and short stories. In these we can find, under many disguises, much that is autobiographical, and if we know something about his life it becomes easier to realise the full significance of the struggles of Jude Fawley, Tess Durbeyfield and the others.

People usually come to Hardy in exactly the reverse order of these three ways. They may be studying one of his novels, they may have read one or two others, they may then come across his poems and finally they may learn a little about his life. This is entirely as it should be. It is, naturally, his written work that is worth studying and the texts of his fiction and his poems are the beginning and end of this study. Putting these texts together into some sort of order will help the reader to see their significance more clearly, and a good way of doing this is to use the personal and biographical element as a series of clues to work out an order. Taking *Jude the Obscure* as an example, we are given clues as to Hardy's sympathies towards the hero when we learn that one of Hardy's grandfathers was a builder while the other was something of a wastrel, that Hardy's father was in the building trade, too, that Hardy himself was an architect who was engaged for a time on church restoration, that he once thought of going into the church and that at the same time as he was engaged in restoring the physical fabric of the churches he was losing faith in the beliefs of the church itself.

These however are only clues, signposts towards the texts themselves, and biographical detail can never be quoted as *proof* that a particular text means something; meanings can only be discovered in the texts themselves. We can, however, pick up some of the main themes that run through Hardy's work by discovering their probable origins in his life.

Dorset, 1840

Hardy was born in Lower Bockhampton, Dorset, in 1840. It was, and is, just a collection of houses rather than a village, and its life is orientated towards the nearby village of Stinsford, where Hardy went to church and where he is now buried, and towards Dorchester, the county town, three miles away. His father was a fairly prosperous builder and his mother a well-read woman who had known poverty as the daughter of a labourer and shepherd in uncertain employment.

It was still the old world. Hardy was to live to see motor-cars, aeroplanes and tanks, Freudianism and neurosurgery, telephones and radios, but his origins are in the old world of the English countryside: cottage, farm labourer, milkmaid, squire, market town, and country lore. This is the world (seen in its purest form in *Under the Greenwood Tree*) which forms the matrix of his fiction and which he transformed into the half-real half-mythical 'Wessex' shown on a map at the beginning of all his novels. It is a region probed by the modern world, by railways and corn drills (in *The Mayor of Casterbridge*) and by threshing machines (in *Tess*) and it is a world on whose edges is to be felt a touch of the urban and industrial in the shape of London and, in *Jude* for instance, Reading ('Aldbrickham' as it is so carefully called). But for all this it remains the old world in which ordinary people travel on foot just as Hardy walked the three miles into Dorchester every day both as a schoolboy and later as an architect's apprentice. It is the world of agricultural pursuits in which the machine is alien, a world of peasant fatalism and simple pleasures but also – and this is important for Hardy's purposes as a novelist – it is a world dominated by the chances of nature which the modern world has managed to some extent to control. Thus a storm (in *Far From the Madding Crowd*) or a wild fluctuation in the price of corn (in *The Mayor of Casterbridge*) or a snake-bite (in *The Return of the Native*) can inexorably change the lives of the inhabitants of Wessex.

Dorset in 1840, the basic model of Hardy's dream-kingdom of Wessex, is also 'old' in the sense that it is provincial, rural and backward. In the novels London, and even Oxford, function in much the same way as nature does, that is, capriciously and often with disastrous results. In *The Woodlanders*, for instance, a Wessex lawyer thinks that a new divorce law may have come into force and Mr Melbury goes to London to find out about it, but the information was inaccurate (the 'lawyer' is only a clerk) and the powers that rule the law, like the powers that rule nature, turn out to have decreed something different from what Melbury expects, so his daughter Grace cannot be divorced from her faithless husband and cannot marry the man she loves. London law is here as unpredictable as the weather.

In 1883 Hardy wrote 'The Dorsetshire Labourer', an essay which describes something of the conditions of the common man in this older world. In spite of the fatalism and the primitive conditions under which such people lived Hardy envied them (as must be apparent from the attractive and cheerful 'rustic choruses' he includes in novels such as *Far From the Madding Crowd* and *Under the Greenwood Tree*). In his essay he wrote that 'it is among such communities as these that happiness will find her last refuge on earth, since it is among them that a perfect insight into the conditions of existence will be longest postponed.'

Out of the old world of Dorset and its surrounding counties, then, Hardy fashioned the tragedies of his Wessex, and it is clear that there was material for tragedy to hand. But he did not suggest that a new world would do much to alleviate matters: it could in fact make them worse (Donald Farfrae is more modern than Mayor Henchard in *The Mayor of Casterbridge*, and he contributes directly to the latter's ruin; Alec D'Urberville is a brash modern man with an industrial fortune behind him) and, anyway, the essay argues that modern thinking would only give people a better 'insight' into the 'conditions of existence'. Hardy assumes that, both in the old world and in the new, there is little to be enjoyed and much to be endured.

Young Hardy

Hardy did not go to a famous school or to university, but he was well educated. His mother introduced him to serious reading early (she gave him Dryden's translation of Virgil at the age of eight, for example) and he went to quite a good school in Dorchester from 1849 to 1856, that is, between the ages of nine and sixteen. He learnt Latin and other school subjects but the real development of his mind, not surprisingly, seems to have started when he left school and was articled to the Dorchester architect, John Hicks. He worked in Hicks's office

PLATE 1: Thomas Hardy, a portrait photograph taken in about 1885.

for five years (1856-61) and during that time, besides learning the rudiments of architecture and discussing all manner of things with his fellow pupils, he taught himself Greek, started to write poetry, met the Dorset poet William Barnes (1801-86) and came under the influence of Horace Moule (1832-73), son of the vicar of a nearby village, who introduced him to some of the more modern trends of thought including the work of Charles Darwin (1809-82), whose theory of evolution expounded in his work *On the Origin of Species* caused so great a commotion on its publication in 1859.

The next five years (1862-7) completed Hardy's education. During this period he was in London where he worked for the architect Arthur Blomfield. Here, of course, he was able to add experience of the metropolis (dancing in tea-rooms, visiting the National Gallery) to his deep knowledge of the country, and to continue his programme of wide reading. In particular his religious faith was profoundly shaken during this time (it was never to recover although he later described himself, accurately, as 'churchy') and he became an agnostic. Most crucial of all, he began to discover the torments of love.

As far as Hardy's loss of faith goes, we can do worse than to look at his early poems, 'Hap' and 'The Impercipient'. 'Hap' proposes the notion that underpins all Hardy's work: that Nature, or Fate, or the Universe, is neither hostile nor favourable to man, but indifferent:

> If but some vengeful god would call to me
> From up the sky, and laugh: 'Thou suffering thing,
> Know that thy sorrow is my ecstasy,
> That thy love's loss is my hate's profiting!'
>
> Then would I bear it, clench myself, and die,
> Steeled by the sense of ire unmerited;
> Half-eased in that a Powerfuller than I
> Had willed and meted me the tears I shed.
>
> But not so. How arrives it joy lies slain,
> And why unblooms the best hope ever sown?
> —Crass Casualty obstructs the sun and rain,
> And dicing Time for gladness casts a moan . . . .
> These purblind Doomsters had as readily strown
> Blisses about my pilgrimage as pain.

'The Impercipient' looks not at the gods but at men in church and wistfully wishes for faith:

> Upon them stirs in lippings mere
> (As if once clear in call,
> But now scarce breathed at all)—
> 'We wonder, ever wonder, why we find us here'

As for love, there are scores of poems to be quoted, and love, especially the failures and pains of passion, is the constant point around which his novels revolve.

Hardy was extremely susceptible to beautiful women, and he seems to have been capable of a remarkable, if delayed, fidelity to his memories and feelings about them. At the age of fifteen he fell in love, briefly, with one Louisa Harding; at eighty-seven he wrote the nostalgic love poem 'To Louisa in the Lane'.

> Meet me again as at that time
>   In the hollow of the lane;
> I will not pass as in my prime
>   I passed at each day's wane.
>   —Ah, I remember!
> To do it you will have to see
> Anew this sorry scene wherein you have ceased to be!

When in London he seems to have run the gamut of emotions about the opposite sex, with an emphasis on disappointment if the 'She, to Him' sonnets of this period, or 'Revulsion' (also dated 1866) are a reliable guide. On returning to Dorset in 1867 he met and probably fell in love with his cousin, Tryphena Sparks; perhaps they had an affair during the years 1867-9; perhaps the gloomy poem 'Neutral Tones' of 1867 refers to this liaison; perhaps the equally gloomy 'At Rushy-Pond' refers to the end of the affair. If so, Hardy's pessimistic view of love was much strengthened, and, once again, we find little reference to this painful relationship until many years later when Hardy unaccountably calls one of the d'Urberville chickens in *Tess* (1891) 'Phena' and then refers to 'the death of a woman' (in a context which implies Tryphena) in the Preface to *Jude the Obscure* (1895). We cannot be sure of the facts in all this. Hardy was always a secretive man (and his secretiveness was surely a measure of his sensitivity) and we get no more than glimpses of the sufferings of a young man in love as fragments of old emotions resurface decades later in ambiguous but moving verses.

By 1869, then, when he was twenty-nine, we might consider Hardy's apprenticeship to life complete. By then he had written his first novel, later destroyed, *The Poor Man and the Lady*, and by the age of thirty we can think of him, living in Dorset again, a trained architect, a poet, a well-read man, experienced in the ways of love, an aspiring novelist. By this same year of 1870 he had developed his own idiosyncratic view of the world which was not to change much in the fifty-eight years which lay before him. His remarkable and delayed fidelity to the memory of women was paralleled by a remarkable consistency of ideas; he saw life steadily and he saw it whole, and as he went on to fame (and notoriety) and some fortune he remained the amalgam of countryman, humorist, Darwinian intellectual and pessimist about love that he had become by 1870.

Hardy the novelist

The Poor Man and the Lady was not entirely lost. Part of it reappeared in *Under the Greenwood Tree* and part as the long short story *An Indiscretion in the Life of an Heiress* (1878). It is clear from these fragments that Hardy saw himself as a poor man who aspired to the hand of a 'lady'; the novel seems to explore Hardy's own fascination with upper-class life in general and upper-class women in particular. Anyone reading his autobiography is struck by how much of it is devoted to descriptions of the grand dinner-parties of the London 'Season' and of the frequent contacts with the upper classes which Hardy made, once he had become famous. Apart from the fact that in Victorian England success was always equated with an upward move in the class system, there was in Hardy's case the special impression made on him by the beautiful and sophisticated Julia Martin who lived in a splendid Georgian house at Kingston Maurward near Bockhampton between 1845 and 1855 and took an interest in his progress when he was a child. The poem 'Amabel' describes Hardy's disappointment at discovering how she had aged when he visited her in London in 1865.

> I marked her ruined hues,
> Her custom-straitened views
> And asked, 'Can therein dwell
> My Amabel?'
>
> I looked upon her gown,
> Once rose, now earthen brown,
> The change was like the knell
> Of Amabel.

It proved difficult to find a publisher for this sort of poem, and the poor man, if he was to get into print and to impress the 'ladies', had to turn to fiction. His first attempt was rejected: *The Poor Man and the Lady* was read in manuscript by two eminent Victorians, the editor and critic John Morley (1838-1923) and novelist and poet George Meredith (1828-1909), and criticised adversely. Following this criticism to the letter, Hardy decided to try something more sensational. This was *Desperate Remedies* and it was while he was writing this rather improbable and overwrought tale that he met and at once fell in love with his future wife, Emma Gifford. In his capacity as an architect Hardy had been sent to explore the possibility of restoring a much dilapidated church in Cornwall, at St Juliot, where Emma Gifford was staying at the time with her sister and brother-in-law, the vicar of the St Juliot parish. Ironically, perhaps, this meeting inspired two sets of poems. The first, including 'When I set Out for Lyonnesse' and 'The Wind's Prophecy', were written at the time. Emma's death, more than forty years later, was the occasion for the second set which includes Hardy's greatest love poems ('Poems 1912-1913') written in a burst of remorse and remembering. These poems are the most striking example of Hardy's capacity for the re-creation of emotion many years later. It is ironic that Emma, who indirectly inspired Hardy to write poetry, assisted him directly in the preparation of *Desperate Remedies* for the publisher and helped him with other novels. Their marriage (1874-1912) was in fact the period of Hardy's life principally devoted to his career as a novelist.

It was not a happy marriage. Emma believed that a Divine Providence ruled her ways while Hardy saw men as the 'bond-servants of Chance' ('Ditty') and their views of the world were utterly opposed. Emma, who was often ill and with whose sufferings Hardy failed to sympathise, became difficult and proud, finally somewhat eccentric; Hardy withdrew into himself, ever one for concealment and retreat; there were no children; in the 1890s Hardy added an outside staircase to his house, Max Gate in Dorchester, so that he could move between his study and the garden without, it was said, encountering Emma.

But for Hardy all this may have been a blessing. Out of his Cornish romance he was able to build a personal mythology from which great poetry sprang; he referred to the spectacular coastline near St Juliot as a 'place pre-eminently (for one person at least) the region of dream and mystery'. Just as 'Wessex' is a dream version of the real Dorset so Hardy may have based dreams of passion on the unsatisfactory reality of his marriage. The very unsatisfactoriness may have been what made this possible: if he had been contented he might not have felt driven to re-create the world anew in his fiction. His heart remained open to new loves and he continued to feel those emotions from which literature is born far later in life than most people. He states this directly in the brief but moving poem 'I Look Into My Glass':

I look into my glass,
And view my wasting skin,
And say, 'Would God it came to pass
My heart had shrunk as thin!'

For then, I, undistrest,
By hearts grown cold to me,
Could lonely wait my endless rest
With equanimity.

But Time, to make me grieve,
Part steals, lets part abide;
And shakes this fragile frame at eve
With throbbings of noontide.

One of the clearest clues to understanding Hardy's career as a poet lies here. Most lyric poets have written their best work by the time they are thirty-five; Hardy wrote a good deal of poetry as a young man, too, but he wrote a lot more in his sixties and seventies and eighties. He claimed that he was a young man until he was forty, but perhaps he was in some respects a young man all his life.

Hardy and Emma married in 1874 and at first they moved from one place to another—Surbiton, Sturminster Newton, London, Wimborne Minster—but in 1883 they moved to Dorchester (the 'Casterbridge' of the novels) and started to build a house, Max Gate, designed by Hardy himself, into which they finally settled in 1885. By now Hardy was famous and financially comfortable and he and Emma spent a good part of each year in London, where they were taken up by fashionable society and where they met other writers. The story of the years from 1870, when they first met, to 1897, is the story of Hardy's career as a novelist, from *Desperate Remedies*, published in 1871, to *The Well-Beloved* of 1897, his last published novel.

This career had its contradictions and ambiguities and, like all other aspects of Hardy's life, shows signs of concealment and opposing forces. The man who was of humble origins dined at the best tables; the man who fell in love with Emma Gifford lived to regret his marriage, to write bitterly against marriage as an institution, and to celebrate his early romance decades after it occurred in great poems such as that opening 'Woman much missed, how you call to me, call to me'; the great novelist wanted to be a great poet. As a novelist Hardy claimed once that he wanted merely to be thought 'a good hand at a serial' but went on to write some of the greatest novels of the nineteenth century, and not by accident either; it is clear that his major work is profoundly heartfelt and carefully constructed. At the same time he produced some less than satisfactory minor novels and was able, in preparing the complete 'Wessex' edition of his fiction, to divide them more or less as later critics have done. Hardy's own divisions (which include his short stories as well) are these:

I. Novels of Character and Environment

1. *Tess of the D'Urbervilles*
2. *Far from the Madding Crowd*
3. *Jude the Obscure*
4. *The Return of the Native*
5. *The Mayor of Casterbridge*

6. *The Woodlanders*
7. *Under the Greenwood Tree*
8. *Life's Little Ironies*
9. *Wessex Tales*

II. Romances and Fantasies

10. *A Pair of Blue Eyes*
11. *The Trumpet-Major*
12. *Two on a Tower*
13. *The Well-Beloved*
14. *A Group of Noble Dames*

III. Novels of Ingenuity

15. *Desperate Remedies*
16. *The Hand of Ethelberta*
17. *A Laodicean*

IV. Mixed Novels

18. *A Changed Man, The Waiting Supper and Other Tales,* concluding with the *Romantic Adventures of a Milkmaid*

It can be seen from this list that Hardy wrote both major and minor fiction throughout his career. The actual chronology of the novels is as follows:

1871 *Desperate Remedies*
1872 *Under the Greenwood Tree*
1873 *A Pair of Blue Eyes*
1874 *Far From the Madding Crowd*
1876 *The Hand of Ethelberta*
1878 *The Return of the Native*
1880 *The Trumpet-Major*
1881 *A Laodicean*
1882 *Two on a Tower*
1886 *The Mayor of Casterbridge*
1887 *The Woodlanders*
1891 *Tess of the d'Urbervilles*
1882 (and 1897) *The Well-Beloved*
1895 *Jude the Obscure*

For more than a quarter of a century, then, Hardy wrote novels (and short stories) for a living. Most of them are set earlier in the century than the date of their composition, often in the 1830s, 1840s and 1850s. This reminds us that Hardy's roots are in the old Dorset of his parents' stories and of his own early years and that his magic country of Wessex, once again, cannot be equated with the 'modern' world in which Hardy was actually writing. Casterbridge, for instance, is an idealised version of the semi-rural town he knew as a boy, it is not the Dorchester in which he lived (in a somewhat urban house) from 1885. The divorce legislation that plays such a part in *The Woodlanders* is not the legislation of the 1890s but that of the 1850s; examples abound of Hardy's habit of reaching back in time for the substance of his novels.

Hardy the poet

Hardy was writing poetry as early as the 1860s. 'Amabel', his earliest dated poem, was written in 1865 and, besides that, there is the poem 'Domicilium' written 'between 1857 and 1860'; the latter is a talented youthful piece describing, typically for Hardy, both what the cottage at Bockhampton looked like in 1857, and what it had been like forty years before he was even born, when his grandparents first moved there. This early poem is a fascinating, if rather formal, glimpse into Hardy's mind as an adolescent.

The poems of the 1860s, obviously products of the fervours of early manhood, are many of them quite remarkable, but it remains a fact that Hardy did not *publish* any poetry until 1898 when his *Wessex Poems* began his thirty-year career as a published poet.

The events of this later period in Hardy's life include his writing *The Dynasts*, a culmination of his lifelong fascination with the period of the Napoleonic wars, a massive verse drama that serves as a sort of poetic film-script laying out all of Europe beneath us, considering it from the point of view of the immortal gods and then focusing on detailed scenes where individuals decide the fate of the masses that populate the wider scenes. *The Dynasts* occupied Hardy between 1902 and 1907 and it must have seemed like his final statement on the way the universe works, but there was the First World War (1914-18) still to come and when it came Hardy, who had thought and written about war during the South African campaign of 1899-1901 (in such poems as 'Drummer Hodge') found that such small elements of hope as seemed available to man were taken from him. After 1918, he said, he was no longer an 'evolutionary meliorist', that is, he could no longer believe that evolution was leading man away from barbaric times and towards comfort, justice and happiness.

Before the war, in 1912, Emma had died and the great sequence 'Poems 1912-1913' was written; in 1914 he married Florence Dugdale, who had been his secretary and who was to become the nominal authoress of his autobiography. The photographs show Florence to have been an attractive woman and one is tempted to speculate about the 'throbbings of noontide' that filled his 'fragile frame' when he married a much younger woman during the 'eve' of his life (he was

PLATE 2: A drawing of Thomas Hardy made by William Strang (1859-1921) at Max Gate in 1910, when Hardy was aged seventy.

seventy-four, she was forty-two). We cannot, however, even begin to assess the relationship between this emotion and the profound regret and nostalgia that had followed Emma's death. Hardy remained secretive and enigmatic as ever. Neither from this period, nor from his youth do we have any photographs of Hardy smiling. After his death Florence supervised the burning of a mass of paper from his study; no doubt there were letters, diaries, perhaps poems, destroyed in that bonfire that would have shed light on the emotional life of this passionate but reticent man.

The chronology of Hardy's published poetry is as follows:

1898 *Wessex Poems*
1901 *Poems of the Past and the Present*
1909 *Time's Laughingstocks*
1914 *Satires of Circumstance*
1917 *Moments of Vision*
1922 *Late Lyrics and Earlier*
1925 *Human Shows*
1928 *Winter Words*

The second half of Hardy's literary career, then, was that of poet. It is worth remembering that these thirty years (1898-1928) cover the main part of the literary period we have come to call 'Modernist'. That is to say, Hardy, the Victorian novelist, is also, as a poet, the contemporary of such Modernist poets as T.S. Eliot (1888-1965), Ezra Pound (1885-1972) and W.B. Yeats (1865-1939). Eliot's *Prufrock* appeared in 1917 and is regarded as a distinctive break with the older and more conventional poetry of the Victorian and Edwardian periods. It appears to have had no influence on Hardy at all. In most respects Hardy seems to belong to the pre-Modernist period, to be a Victorian voice lingering on into the twentieth century, and this is perhaps not surprising. After all, most of his great poems date from the 1860s, the 1870s and from 1912-13. But if we look at the development of poetry since the Second World War, it becomes apparent that the Modernist voice is not the only one to be heard in this century. The poems of R. S. Thomas (*b.* 1913) or Philip Larkin (*b.* 1922) or Ted Hughes (*b.* 1930), for instance, show a personal and simple touch or a direct involvement with nature that derive from Hardy rather than T.S. Eliot. This realisation can help us to see Hardy as an alternative to Modernism and to see also what it is in him that separates him from his Victorian contemporaries. He does not make the music of a Tennyson (1809-92) or a Swinburne (1837-1909) nor does he have the firm rhythmic structure of an Arnold (1822-88) or the capacity to present complex thought of a Browning (1812-89). He is, it seems, a new voice, not as radically new as the Modernists and yet not really a mainstream

Victorian. He is his own man, writing in his own intensely personal voice, and he is, at his best, a great poet.

Hardy died peacefully in January 1928. In the last months of his life he spent much time recollecting his earliest years, over the fire in the evening, with Florence. Indeed, he had dictated a two-volume autobiography to her and, as ever, it was out of the past that he created his present mythology. The autobiography conceals much of the reality of his life and may count, perhaps, as his last work of fiction. Before he died Hardy asked Florence to read him a stanza from *Omar Khayyam* by Edward Fitzgerald (1809-83):

> Thou, who Man of baser Earth didst make
> And who with Eden didst devise the Snake;
> For all the Sin wherewith the Face of man
> Is blacken'd, Man's Forgiveness give—and take!

His last thoughts, it seems, were humble but proud, humane but challenging, ambiguous as ever. He died as he had lived.

Chapter 2

The main themes of Hardy's writing

The intellectual climate of Hardy's early life

In the second half of the nineteenth century, that is from the time that Hardy was ten until the time he was sixty, the sciences as we know them today came into being. The eighteenth century may have been the 'Age of Reason' and the early nineteenth century may have provided the technology that made the Industrial Revolution possible but, as we saw when discussing Dorset in 1840, the 'old world' persisted well into the nineteenth century and the intellectual climate of the first half of the century was not seriously affected by science. Of course there are individual exceptions but if we look at the beginning of the nineteenth century and compare it with its closing years we are struck by the immense contrast. Between 1800 and 1900, the sciences of sociology and psychology, of geology and palaeontology, of archaeology and anthropology were virtually invented. What was medicine or astronomy or biology or even physics and chemistry in 1800 compared to what they had become by 1900?

Science aspires to be an objective, dispassionate study of the natural world and its inhabitants. It is concerned not with how things should be or might be but only with how things are. In this sense Hardy was the child of his time, the product of the scientific view that was developing throughout his lifetime. As an example, we can look at the way the idea of 'nature' changed before and during the nineteenth century. In the seventeenth and eighteenth centuries nature was perceived in terms of a 'pastoral' convention, it was formalised and to some extent trivialised. Wordsworth (1770-1850) and the Romantics, at the beginning of the nineteenth century, took nature more seriously but their concern was with the inspiration it afforded the artist (Wordsworth's 'Tintern Abbey', for example, or Coleridge's (1772-1834) 'Frost at Midnight') or the sheer sensuous beauty of it (Keats's (1795-1821) 'To Autumn'). What Hardy added to this was the scientific view, especially as formulated by Charles Darwin.

Hardy sees nature not just as landscape or background, nor as a source of inspiration and beauty but more deeply and completely as a whole web of blind forces thrusting forward in an inexorable movement. This, of course, is Darwin's 'Struggle for Life' as outlined in his *On the Origin of Species* (1859). In that year Hardy was nineteen and, like Darwin himself, had spent years in the close inspection of nature. Darwin was initiated into the study of nature by a Cambridge tutor and then spent five years (1833-8) aboard HMS *Beagle* voyaging round South America and visiting every kind of physical environment that that continent has to offer. Hardy had nature thrust upon him, as it were, in the rural surroundings of his childhood; there was no escape, in Bockhampton, from wind and weather, from animals and vegetables, from the powerful annual cycle of country life. Darwin became a great scientist and proposed the theory of the evolution of species through time; in the struggle for life the fittest would survive and breed while the less fit would become extinct; in the natural world there was no benign plan, indeed hardly a plan at all, the conditions produced the species and, as the conditions changed, the species had to change too, or perish.

Hardy became a great novelist by dramatising these same insights. For him, as for the scientist, things were as they were, not because God had planned them thus nor because man, by transgression, had spoilt the plan, but because that was how the blind forces of nature (the 'purblind doomsters' of the sonnet 'Hap') had happened to work. Darwin's work caused a sensation, not to say a scandal, partly because it implied that, just as there was no divine origin for species, so there was no divine origin for man, in fact, man was just another species, a highly developed ape. Exactly this implication is present in Hardy, too. Instead of setting human beings against a separate background of nature Hardy presses man and nature together in his Darwinian mould. This union with nature is frequently symbolised in the novels: Diggory Venn, in *The Return of the Native* covers himself in the turves of Egdon Heath in order to conceal himself; Clym Yeobright, in the same novel, is reduced to the level and status of a heath creature in a marvellous and moving passage (Book 4, Chapter 2). Giles Winterborne, in *The Woodlanders*, is 'autumn's very brother' and, in the same novel, Little Hintock is lost in the woods and dominated by the trees to the point of claustrophobia. Tess Durbeyfield is '*made*' of the milk and honey on which she mostly lives and, far from being an identifiable human being set against the landscape in which she moves, is like 'a fly on a billiard table' or a speck on the fields at Flintcomb-Ash.

As in nature, so in man's life. Hardy is aware of the struggle for life taking place equally in both spheres and he works out a kind of applied Darwinism whereby the laws of evolution are seen to operate on man in the same way as they operate on nature.

Darwinism was, of course, not the only thing happening in the intellectual life of the 1850s, 1860s and 1870s. It was a time of religious controversy as well and, although some of this controversy stemmed directly from the advances of science, much of it did not. The question of Catholicism, in one form or another, recurred constantly between 1820 and 1870; at first it was the question of 'emancipation' (the question was whether Catholics should be allowed to hold public office, stand for Parliament, and so on). This was settled by the Act of 1829. Then came the Oxford Movement (1833-46 approximately) which sought to re-establish a quasi-Catholic orthodoxy in the Church of England; this 'High Church' movement came increasingly to the notice of the public and there was something of a scandal when its acknowledged leader, Newman, joined the Catholic Church in 1845. But in 1851 the Catholic hierarchy was re-established in England and Wales and there were once again Catholic bishops, and even cardinals, in Britain. For the next twenty years at least the controversies over how Catholic the Anglican Church should be, and how Catholics should be treated, rumbled on.

At the other end of the scale there was the 'Low Church', the earnest Evangelicals who made up that wing of the Church of England most opposed to Rome. Beyond the Low Church were the Dissenters, Methodists, Baptists and the like in their varying degrees of austerity.

Some of this appears in Hardy's life and writings. It is known that during the time he was apprenticed to the Dorchester architect John Hicks in the late 1850s he engaged in religious debate with his fellow apprentices, particularly on the question of infant baptism. His novels show some interest in such discussions, usually when clergymen are involved, especially in *A Laodicean*. Some of the action of *Under the Greenwood Tree* revolves around the vicar, Mr Maybold, and in *Tess of the d'Urbervilles* and *Jude the Obscure* a series of theological points are raised that remind us of the religious controversies of Hardy's youth. Tess's baptism of Sorrow, her baby, is discussed from the point of view of its validity, Angel Clare's brothers are somewhat satirical portraits of the earnest young clergymen of the 1860s and 70s, Angel's father is an Evangelical of the old school, and so on. Jude Fawley considers becoming some sort of priest or preacher, Arabella flirts with a Dissenting sect (as did Alec d'Urberville, we remember) and the whole matter of the relationship of the Church of England to the University at Christminster (Oxford) is present in a shadowy form below the surface of the novel.

The main religious controversy of the time, however, concerned the reaction to scientific discovery and hypothesis. How was the Church to take Darwin? How was it to take the new critical approach to the Bible? Scientists, archaeologists and literary historians had for half a century thrown doubt on the authenticity of parts of Scripture and had questioned the historical reality of much of it, including the story of Christ himself. If the Bible was only a book like any other, if it too was subject to the cool scrutiny of science, where was a man to look for truth? To science itself, perhaps, or, in other words, to nature? But Darwin had taken God out of nature, too.

On the Origin of Species had appeared in 1859. In 1860 there appeared *Essays and Reviews*, a volume of seven pieces by senior Anglicans which argued for some sort of accommodation to be reached between the Church and the scientists (biblical critics and evolutionists for the most part). The more conservative element in the Church of England dubbed the seven contributors the 'Septem Contra Christum', the 'Seven Against Christ', and a collection of *Replies to Essays and Reviews* was published. It is this restatement of the traditional opinions, disguised as '*A Counterblast to Agnosticism*', that the Clare brothers are reading in *Tess of the d'Urbervilles*.

Other Victorian writers show signs of a crisis of faith as well as Hardy; indeed, nearly all the main literary figures of the period are uneasy about religion. Dickens (1812-1870) and Thackeray (1811-1863) each held to a somewhat personal form of Christianity of their own but Tennyson came very close indeed to losing his faith (see the evolutionary anxieties of *In Memoriam*, for instance), Matthew Arnold, in 'Dover Beach' and the 'Marguerite' poems, stressed man's isolation and faithless helplessness, Browning was drawn to unbelief while George Eliot (1819-1880) was a professed agnostic. Many minor but influential figures were also vociferous in their attacks on established religion. Darwin's exponent, T.H. Huxley (1825-1895), preached science and rationalism in lectures and essays; Arthur Clough (1819-1861) speculated about the meaning of Easter and rewrote the Ten Commandments in ironic vein; Leslie Stephen (1832-1904) abandoned Holy Orders, and Hardy, in a curious episode, was asked to witness Stephen's signature on the document needed for this.

Hardy, then, lived in a world of religious controversy in which, inspite of the assaults it had to sustain, religion showed itself to be extremely vigorous. It has been demonstrated, for instance, that it was only in the 1870s, when Hardy was establishing himself as a novelist, that the number of novels being published each year began to equal, and eventually to outstrip, the number of religious texts of one kind or another. Meanwhile science advanced apace. Religion and science are perhaps the keys to the intellectual background to Hardy's writings.

Wessex

In the discussion of Hardy's early life, in the first chapter above, Wessex was called a 'dream kingdom'. It was a dream that came to him slowly. In *The Poor Man and the Lady* and in his first published novel, *Desperate Remedies*, there is not the concentration on place of which Hardy was later to become a master. We do not know the full details of the plot of *The Poor Man and the Lady* (the manuscript was destroyed) but it was criticised by the publisher's reader for being politically inflammatory and it appears to have been set partly at least in London. *Desperate Remedies*, as far as its setting goes, is a rural novel but it concentrates on sensational events and complex plot at the expense of country life. In *Under the Greenwood Tree* we have a delightful and entirely natural description of Dorset, but only with the Preface to *Far From the Madding Crowd* do we find Hardy self-consciously employing the term 'Wessex'. As the series of novels progressed he became caught up in this creation of his and began to provide maps of 'Wessex' and to use the name more frequently; this process culminated in the title of his first volume of verse (*Wessex Poems*, 1898), his first volume of short stories (*Wessex Tales*, 1888) and the collected edition of his fiction (the 'Wessex Edition' of 1912). But not all of Hardy is caught up in Wessex, for all that this was the name he gave to his favourite dog, and, although it is sometimes reasonable when discussing Hardy's work to speak of him as the Wessex poet and novelist, it is worth noticing that he once thought of writing social (or perhaps 'society') novels and that he seemed always to have half an eye on a different sort of people and on the world outside Wessex.

Thus, in *The Woodlanders* for instance, we encounter Mrs Charmond who belongs less to Wessex than she does to her German 'watering place', and Dr Fitzpiers who is an alien being destined, according to the locals at Hintock, to an early departure. It may be objected that Mrs Charmond does, after all, possess an old manor house in or near the village and that Fitzpiers comes from an important local family. But that would be to miss the point about Wessex—it is an idea as much as a place, and it is an idea which, although it contains a strong class element, excludes the upper classes. It is because Mrs Charmond and Fitzpiers are educated upper-class people, *gentry*, that they do not seem to belong. They can be as much at home in London or in Europe as in Hintock, indeed, rather more so. This is something characteristic of Hardy: throughout the eighteenth and nineteenth centuries novels were largely concerned with the upper, or at least the middle classes; in Hardy, however, we find few polite drawing-rooms and as his novels progress he seems less and less tempted to enter that well-trodden arena. Of course there are characters in Dickens from all classes but they are treated unequally; the upper-class characters in his novels have the power and position of their equivalents in real life while the lower-class characters are seen from the point of view of an educated narrator. Hardy moves down the scale somewhat. He can

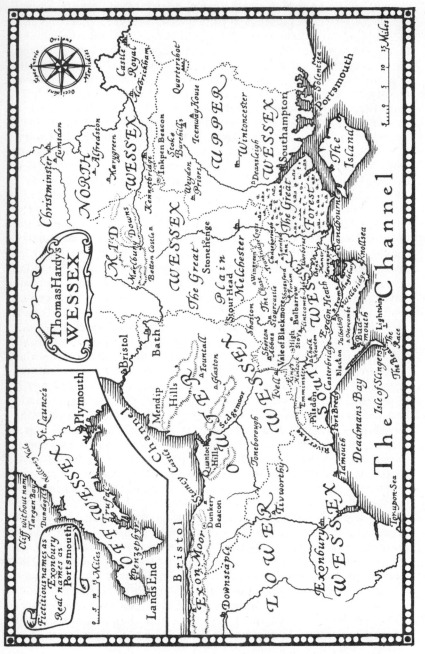

PLATE 3: A map showing the fictional and real names of places that feature in Hardy's Wessex (not one of his own maps).

still treat the 'rustic choruses' of his earlier fiction from a superior point of view (*Far From the Madding Crowd* with its Joseph Poorgrass and Henery Fraye seems to be the best example here) but he can enter into the lives of people almost as humble as these on terms of equality. Thus Gabriel Oak (in *Far From the Madding Crowd*) is a small farmer turned shepherd, Clym Yeobright (in *The Return of the Native*) a shop worker, a furze cutter and a lowly preacher, Michael Henchard (in *The Mayor of Casterbridge*) is a farm worker and a grain dealer. There is something more to each of these unpromising people, of course, and Hardy makes a lot of that something more: Clym's shop experience is gained in a jeweller's shop in Paris, which is not like selling shoes in Casterbridge; Gabriel Oak is intelligent, resourceful, capable of being a farm manager; Henchard becomes the Mayor of Casterbridge. These are not *gentry*, but Hardy does not talk down to them, he takes them, on the whole, seriously, and perhaps that is not to be wondered at when we remember his own social origins. He was fascinated by the upper classes, and delighted in fashionable London dinner parties, but his roots were firmly in a lower class and it is among this class that his dramas were played out. As he says of Little Hintock early in *The Woodlanders*: 'It was one of those sequestered spots outside the gates of the world . . . where, from time to time, dramas of a grandeur and unity truly Sophoclean are enacted in the real.'

The dream kingdom of Wessex, then, is set apart from the fashionable life of London and the upper classes. It turns its back on such scenes as much as on the industrial and urban world of Victorian Britain. Other novelists such as Mrs Gaskell (1810-65), in, for example, *North and South* (1855) and George Gissing (1857-1903), in, say, *Workers in the Dawn* (1880), chronicled the struggle of the urban poor, the slum-dwellers produced by the Industrial Revolution. Hardy restricted himself to the rural, the humble, the non-political.

The first image that comes to mind with the word 'Wessex' is one of landscape. The characters of the Wessex novels are profoundly and intimately bound up with their physical environment and we remember the two together: Eustacia Vye on Egdon Heath, Marty South in the Hintock woods, Tess at Talbothays, Jude scaring the crows in farmer Troutham's field. Hardy's use of landscape, and of the rural and agricultural world in general, has never been equalled. Emile Zola (1840-1902) in *La Terre* (1887) comes closer to Hardy than anything else; but in English literature there are no sustained evocations of the countryside that can match Wessex.

Wessex is divided into regions. Not the sub-divisions of Hardy's map, which correspond to the real counties of south-western England (Off-Wessex=Cornwall, and so on) but regions of the mind based on a vague geographical reality. Thus there is Casterbridge (Dorchester) which is a rural idea of a town (although it is not the 'urban opposite' of the countryside). South of Casterbridge is the coast with its idea of luxury, a touch of fashion in Budmouth (Weymouth, George III's 'watering place') and Sandbourne (opulent Bournemouth with its new villas and its faintly Mediterranean climate). North and west of Casterbridge lie a whole range of instructive ideas impressed in landscape. First, Egdon Heath (of *The Return of the Native*) with its 'haggard' countenance and its sombre insistence on the primitive forces that lie beneath all mere building and 'scenery'. There might be some other features similar to Egdon, such as 'the Great Forest' (the New Forest) or 'the Great Plain' (Salisbury Plain). North of Egdon (in the northern half of Dorset) is located the idea of rich, fecund nature, land at its most productive and, in appearance at least, its most benign. Here in the 'Vale of Blackmore' and in the Hintocks there are trees and crops in profusion. The same idea is present west of Casterbridge in the Frome valley where, at Talbothays dairy, Tess finds a lush and satisfying physical life and where Hardy rejoices in describing a fertility so rich that one can almost hear the 'hiss of fertilization'. All of Dorset ('South Wessex') is home territory, with the possible exception of Sandbourne, and it is not possible to divide it up completely into dominant ideas (there are overlaps). A general test of most of these landscapes, however, would be to ask whether they convey benign ideas, as do Weatherbury (*Far From the Madding Crowd*) and Mellstock (*Under the Greenwood Tree*) or malign ones, as do Egdon Heath and Flintcomb-Ash farm.

Once we leave 'South Wessex' the ideas and meanings of the countryside become starker. Cornwall ('Off-Wessex') is the land of romance (in *A Pair of Blue Eyes* and in many poems), Hampshire ('Upper Wessex') is a more sinister place where the Henchard family troubles start (at Weydon Priors), where Sergeant Troy is billetted to the exclusion of poor Fanny Robin (at Quartershot) and where Tess is executed (at Wintoncester gaol). Oxfordshire ('North Wessex') hardly counts as Wessex at all as it is the setting for only one novel—*Jude the Obscure*. Here Hardy is moving away from the old world of deep Wessex and up and out towards the new world—Jude and Sue eventually end up in an almost industrial urban environment in Albrickham (Reading) and Wessex has been left behind.

In studying Hardy, then, the reader is obliged to think about Wessex. It is inevitable that thoughts of the real Dorset, and of the other counties, should come to mind, but we should also recognise the *ideas* and meanings inherent in the landscapes and places of Wessex and see its overall significance. It is a nineteenth-century world of the mind that largely omits some of the most characteristic obsessions of nineteenth-century fiction, the upper classes and industrialisation.

'Character and Environment'

Hardy divided his novels into three categories of which the first, 'Character and Environment', is clearly meant to include his most substantial fiction. It is worth noticing that Hardy chose these particular words to describe his main novels. He chose to draw our attention to his Darwinism, his humanism, and to Wessex. 'Environment' means Wessex, and it also carries a scientific connotation: it is within, and against, their environment that species must struggle for life. 'Character' indicates Hardy the psychologist, the humanist interested in 'poor hard-run humanity', and balances 'environment' in a way that reminds us that men are not only given a set of circumstances *in* which to live but also a set of personal characteristics *with* which to live. Character and environment interact with each other and, as Hardy quotes approvingly in *The Mayor of Casterbridge*, 'character is fate'.

Here, then, we come to a central theme in Hardy—fate, fate in the sense of the given character interacting with the given environment to produce inevitable results. It could be said that most of his fiction, and indeed most of his poetry, is intended as an illustration of the workings of fate. This fate is a Darwinist one: given such and such a species and such and such an environment certain results are bound to follow. Wessex was an excellent choice of setting to illustrate this: in the detail of country life we can see fate working more clearly perhaps than in big cities or in the drawing-rooms of the great. Certainly Wessex, being intensely rural, enabled Hardy to bring together the natural world, where Darwinism is so obviously at work, and the human world where, he seems to say, we only pretend that it is not.

This theme is of great help to us when studying Hardy. We can select any given character, analyse his or her environment and demonstrate how Hardy moves the character and environment together towards the fated conclusion. Take Sergeant Troy, in *Far From the Madding Crowd*, for example. He is given an unstable character, partly for hereditary reasons to do with his dubious birth and aristocratic connexions and partly for environmental reasons to do with his profession as a soldier. The restless and uncertain being created by these forces is perfectly suited for an erratic existence in which chance encounters and random happenings will determine what he does. Thus he has an affair with Fanny Robin, treats her rather casually, offhandedly agrees to marry her but does not do so because, through a chance mistake, she appears late at the church. His volatile character is such that, temporarily, he is more influenced by his feeling of shame in front of the congregation that has witnessed his long wait in the church than by his deeper commitment to Fanny. Then he encounters Bathsheba, utterly by chance—as Hardy is at great pains to point out—and decides to court her, which he does rather casually. When they are married he spends more time and money at the races than on her farm. Then he chances upon the dead Fanny, and his love for her is instantly renewed. He tires of Bathsheba, goes swimming one day, is swept out to sea, is picked up and instantly adopts a new life without, it seems, a backward look at Bathsheba. For fairly superficial reasons he decides, after some years, to return to her and chooses to do so in a theatrical gesture that is just what we might expect from this flashy and erratic character. On claiming Bathsheba again he encounters the jealousy of Boldwood, who shoots him.

In this story the 'environment' provides the turning-points, the moments of decision: Fanny happens to get pregnant; there happens to be an understandable confusion between the churches of All Saints and All Souls; Troy bumps into Bathsheba in a dark wood and, as he happens to be a soldier and wear spurs, he becomes entangled with her clothing so they become perforce better acquainted; when he goes swimming the current happens to be particularly dangerous and it happens that he is not aware of this as he is unfamiliar with that coastline, and so on. But all of this 'environment' would hardly matter were it not for Troy's character: he just is the sort of man who has affairs with girls and gets them pregnant, he is proud and cannot stand the supposed humiliation in the church, he is interested in pretty girls and when he bumps into one, typically, instead of trying to free her dress from his spur, he deliberately makes the entanglement worse so that he can be with her for longer. Similarly, although it is the environment that provides the dangerous current and the chance rescue, it is Troy's character that impels him to take this opportunity of disappearing and starting another life. It is almost as if he is re-born; he starts his new life nearly naked and entirely without possessions.

So the fate that is built into Sergeant Troy (his character) and the fate that befalls him (his environment and its chance patterns) conspire to create his overall destiny. In all this it is the element of chance that has been stressed, and this may seem something of a paradox; character and environment seem 'determined', fixed elements produced by iron chains of cause and effect, and so they are, but what room is then left for chance? Is not everything fated, determined, inevitable? In fact, of course, these are only the two sides of the same coin. Everything in Hardy *is* determined, but from the point of view of the individual to whom a thing happens it makes sense to say that it 'chanced' to be determined in the way it was. For Hardy things *are as they are*—there is no escaping this—yet he insists that it is only a matter of chance that they *are* that way. This will become more intelligible if we consider the painful question of Hardy and God.

Hardy's metaphysics

There is a contradiction in Hardy's work: things are fated and yet random, determined and yet a matter of chance. It needs little demonstration that this *is* Hardy's position; we can, however, take an example from *Tess of the d'Urbervilles* to make the point. Tess, of all people, leads a fated, almost a predestined life; Hardy insists on this at every level: Tess's ancestors have left her the last dregs of decadent aristocratic blood, her pretty face inevitably draws men, even those of a higher class, to take an interest in her, she is the sacrificial victim of tragedy on Stonehenge, she is the Old Testament victim when she exclaims to Alec d'Urberville 'Once victim, always victim. That is the law!' And yet Hardy also stresses the apparently chance nature of her fate. The whole train of events that will lead to Tess being hanged in Wintoncester jail is started by Parson Tringham revealing to Jack Durbeyfield that he is a descendant of the d'Urbervilles who came over with the Conqueror. It is quite by chance that this 'antiquarian' parson has come to live near the Durbeyfields and Tringham himself says to Jack: 'At first I resolved not to disturb you with such a useless piece of information . . . However, our impulses are too strong for our judgement sometimes.' No further explanation is given—it is just an 'impulse' that drives the Parson to speak, and his words are innocent enough, but they lead to the direst of consequences.

Hardy discusses this matter of fate and chance in a number of passages in *Tess of the d'Urbervilles* and extensively at the point, which is our example, where Alec d'Urberville seduces (or rapes) Tess, at the end of 'Phase the First. The Maiden'.

Tess is tired, she has walked miles during the day and has been kept up late, she has narrowly escaped having a fight with the village girls with whom she has been walking home, she has been rescued by Alec on horseback and they have ridden off into woodland, Alec tells her that he has bought her father a new horse that day, they become lost and Tess falls asleep on a pile of dead leaves. Whether with her consent or without it Alec makes love to her. Hardy comments on this event in three paragraphs, which close this 'Phase' of the novel. Here are the essential parts of his commentary.

But, might some say, where was Tess's guardian angel? where was the providence of her simple faith? Perhaps . . . he was talking, or he was pursuing, or he was in a journey, or he was sleeping and not to be awakened.

Why it was that upon this beautiful feminine tissue, sensitive as gossamer, and practically blank as snow as yet, there should have been traced such a coarse pattern as it was doomed to receive; why so often the coarse appropriates the finer thus, the wrong man the woman, the wrong woman the man, many thousand years of analytical philosophy have failed to explain to our sense of order. One may . . . admit the possibility of a retribution lurking in the present catastrophe. Doubtless some of Tess d'Urberville's mailed ancestors rollicking home from a fray had dealt the same measure . . . towards peasant girls of their time . . .

As Tess's own people down in those retreats are never tired of saying . . . in their fatalistic way: 'It was to be.'

In this passage (very useful for any student of Hardy and certainly to be read in its entirety) the novelist considers various possible determining factors that would make sense of Tess's loss of virginity: our guardian angels sometimes stop looking after us, or, alternatively, there is a moral force that brings 'retribution' on people whose ancestors have done wrong. But Hardy does not take these possibilities seriously. The reference to the guardian angel is a joke and the clauses 'he was talking' and 'he was pursuing' are ironical quotations from the Old Testament (I Kings 18:27) where they are also ironical. And after the reference to the 'mailed ancestors' and the possibility of retribution across the generations Hardy comments 'to visit the sins of the fathers upon the children may be a morality good enough for divinities, [but] it is scorned by average human nature.'

The other comments in the passage quoted above are to the effect that, these metaphysical possibilities being laughable, our 'sense of order' simply cannot understand why the wrong people come together and why things are as they are: all we can do is shrug our shoulders and echo 'It was to be.'

In other words, if things were determined by God, if there were a God who arranged when our guardian angels should be on duty or who punished sins on an eye-for-an-eye basis (however unjust) then we would not need to talk of chance. But if there is no ultimate, *metaphysical* reason for things to be as they are then we have to say that, on the deepest level, things are just like that by chance. So we discover that the solution to the paradox Hardy presents between fate and chance is the absence of a divine determiner. Things *are* determined, Hardy provides all the necessary ingredients to make Tess's fate inevitable, but they are not determined for a purpose, only by a chance arrangement of things.

This is the essence of Hardy's metaphysics. It appears time and again in his poems where he often sees humanity as 'God-Forgotten' and describes, movingly, how the world proceeds as though there were an ultimate meaning but how, as far as he can see, there is not.

'Hap' (the poem quoted on p.9) should always be borne in mind when studying Hardy. In his novels there is much of what we can call 'as if' writing; it is 'as if' there is a malign fate pursuing Tess, it is 'as if' the rustics of *Far From the Madding Crowd* are sun-worshippers or nature-worshippers, it is 'as if' the heath-dwellers of *The Return of the Native* are in touch with some ancient pagan power, it is 'as if' nature itself has taken against Giles Winterborne in *The Woodlanders* and 'as if' the gods had set out to thwart Jude Fawley in *Jude the Obscure*. But this is not so. All of these 'as ifs' are merely Hardy's metaphors, employed with a view to emphasising the patterns that govern human existence; the patterns themselves are not divinely inspired, they have no ultimate meaning or significance, in the end there is nobody to blame for the way things are. Thus, statements such as 'Hardy blames Fate' or 'Hardy sees a malign influence at work in the world' should be avoided. Nearly always it would be truer to say, following 'Hap', that although Hardy may play with notions of fate, sacrifice and predestination, what he is in fact illustrating is the mere fact of nature's sheer indifference, the blind forces of chance and evolution governing us without knowing that they do so and without 'meaning' anything. From these metaphysics stems Hardy's compassion: we are all victims together, all in the grip of the same blind forces.

Hardy's ethics

Compassion is a moral or ethical quality, and it is one that Hardy possesses in abundance. As before, we can compare him with Dickens to make the point more clearly. In Dickens there are good and bad characters, that is to say, the problems facing his heroes and heroines are, at least in part, brought about by evil or wicked men. Often these men see the light, change and stop being wicked, but that men can be evil is left in no doubt. Fagin, for instance, in *Oliver Twist*, or Mr Quilp in *The Old Curiosity Shop* or Orlick in *Great Expectations* are figures of evil: they *can* be redeemed, but while they are still unredeemed they are clearly and unquestionably bad.

In Hardy there are no bad men, nor are there even men who go through bad phases. There is no possibility of stopping being wicked in Hardy, no idea of redemption, because his characters are never evil. Indeed, we could say that Hardy's atheist metaphysics leads directly to his ethics of compassion: for him there is no God to test man's soul, no devil to tempt him and possess him with evil; instead, the blind forces of nature and of chance work through him for better or worse. Hardy does not, for instance, blame Alec d'Urberville. Alec is the product of his class, his age, his situation. If a reader parades the other characters from the novels through his or her mind it is soon apparent that none of them is a villain; in one way or other they are all 'natural', they behave as they do because, given their natures and their circumstances, they have no alternative. This tolerance, in which Hardy excels even George Eliot, is a remarkable quality and a sign of an immensely mature vision of the world.

Of course, Hardy is not full of Buddhist resignation. He does not believe that all actions are equal or that no one action is preferable to any other. On the contrary, we can read lessons into Hardy, in particular the lesson of compassion. He does not employ satire to make evil seem grotesque, but prefers to explain all things from their causes and leave us to feel that if we do not like them we can perhaps try to alter the causes rather than blaming the human participants.

One way of understanding the structure of Hardy's fiction, then, is to ask who is to blame for what occurs and then to study the results of that enquiry. It will always turn out that a complete account of the novel has to be given; all the parts of the great web are connected together. Thus, for instance, to follow up our example from *Tess of the d'Urbervilles*, we can argue thus: Alec seems to bear the guilt for Tess's misfortune, but, as we have seen, he is not seriously presented as evil and, anyway, wrong though his action may have been, it was not altogether surprising that he took advantage of the pretty 'cousin' thrust upon him in a position of dependence. Tess's mother, after all, seems to have selected Tess to go and 'claim kin' with Alec on account of her pretty face among other things, and there is an implication that many another village girl would have been delighted to be Alec's mistress (look at the behaviour of Izz Huet and the other girls at Talbothays over Angel Clare). But we cannot stop here and leave it at that. Tess's misfortunes are in part brought about by her own nature and, of course, by Angel. Angel's behaviour should at least set us thinking: if Alec was wrong then so was he; if we had to apportion blame Angel would perhaps deserve it more than Alec. But then we look at the class and religious background in which Angel was brought up and we begin to find excuses for him, too. He was doing a very dangerous thing, socially, in marrying a milkmaid. As a parson, which he might have been, he could have aspired to the hand of a lady and established himself at the top of the social scale; marrying a girl from the very bottom of the scale took a good deal of courage and love. His shock at the revelations of their wedding night is quite genuine – his sleep-walking demonstrates his disturbed state of mind. This leads us to Angel's parents; are they to blame? But when we look at them we find that they are decent, kind people, perhaps a little limited but hardly to be blamed for the predicament in which Angel finds himself.

The argument, if continued, would take us into every detail of the novel; the structure, in other words, is that of a moral web from which blame and guilt are largely excluded. On the other hand, Hardy is clearly moved by compassion, pity and kindness. We react favourably to Tess's care for her family and to her tears as she wrings the necks of the wounded pheasants. We like the parson who does not tell Tess his real views about her baby's possible chances after death, and we like Angel's kindness to her, however belated it may be, when they are at last truly united. To this extent Hardy is a Christian. He believes, like Tess, in 'the spirit of the Sermon on the Mount', that is, he takes from Christianity the central message of humble kindness, of charity. As the world is arranged, he implies, we had better love and help one another if we are to reduce the chances of tragedy. Alec d'Urberville may not be greatly to blame (he appears, particularly in the scene where he makes Tess swear not to 'tempt' him again, in the grip of some alien and powerful force) but it is true that if he had had more consideration for Tess and had thought less selfishly about her she might have escaped the pregnancy and the shame that became so fatal to her.

Thus, beneath the atheist metaphysics and the great determinist web of circumstances which explain and largely excuse action, Hardy retains a quiet Christian voice in which he seems to say that humanity suffers as Christ suffered and that Christ's message of compassion is the most helpful way of living in a difficult world.

Chapter 3

Hardy's techniques

Technique

So far we have concentrated on who Hardy was and on the themes to be found in his writing, themes such as Darwinism, fate and compassion. Now we can examine some of his techniques, that is, some of the ways in which he says what he says, his methods of writing, the 'form' of his works rather than their 'content'.

Hardy was not a Modernist. That is to say, his technique has little in common with the ambiguous or personal or 'difficult' methods of narration of James Joyce (1882-1941) or Virginia Woolf (1882-1941) or D. H. Lawrence (1885-1930). Similarly his poetry has little in common with the experimental, fractured, obscure verse of T. S. Eliot or Ezra Pound. In his novels at least Hardy's technique is Victorian. In other words, he tells a complete and coherent story, without loose ends, in a steady and measured style, taking the fate of the protagonist to a foreseeable end. His novels are highly organised, their structure tightly knit and their tone and style without any marked linguistic surprises. As omniscient narrator Hardy comments on the action or on the setting as he thinks fit, but he tells his stories as though they were objective histories. In this section we shall examine these deceptively conventional aspects of Hardy's novels. The technique of his poetry will be discussed in a separate chapter (Chapter 8, below).

Structure

Hardy said of *Jude the Obscure* that it had an almost 'geometric' plot. We can take this as a clue to his other novels as well and it can help us to see them as the tightly knit structures that they are. Of course the structure is not only evident in the plot; Hardy also carefully controls his setting and symbolism, but we shall start with the plotting.

What Hardy saw in *Jude the Obscure* as 'geometric' is, obviously, the strange square-dance performed by the main characters. Jude makes love to Arabella and is trapped into marrying her; she deserts him and he falls in love with his cousin Sue; Sue marries Phillotson; Sue then deserts Phillotson and goes to live with Jude; Arabella reappears; after the death of the children Sue goes back to Phillotson and Jude fetches up back with Arabella. The neatness of this plot shows Hardy at his most deterministic and, although it has been objected to as somewhat contrived, it greatly increases the power of the determinist vision of the world that the novel seeks to demonstrate.

In the other novels, too, we find a similar technique, this dance performed by the protagonists. In *The Mayor of Casterbridge*, for instance, Michael Henchard is first shown to us at the bottom of the wheel of fortune. He rises to become Mayor, a rich and respected man, but the wheel turns again and he goes down. Donald Farfrae, meanwhile, rises as Henchard falls and, inevitably as we see it, becomes Mayor in his turn. Their relationships with women follow something of the same pattern. Henchard's daughter Elizabeth-Jane and his former girlfriend, Lucetta, are caught up in this pendulum of fortune between the two men. Even a lesser character such as Abel Whittle follows his fate, too, of course, and his life conforms to the pattern of the dance, depending as it does on the attitude towards him, and the power of his employers who are, inevitably, Henchard and Farfrae.

Similarly, in *The Return of the Native*, there is a square-dance between Clym Yeobright and Damon Wildeve and their two partners, Tamsin and Eustacia, with Diggory Venn acting as a sort of master of ceremonies controlling the dance, a referee or umpire. In this example we can see the dynamics of the dance in action in Eustacia. She prefers Clym to Damon because of his Parisian glamour but she fails to appreciate that in the dance of life people are always moving and that, in this case, Clym has decided not to pursue a glamorous career but to become exactly the sort of person Eustacia, in her turn, is trying not to be, a native dweller on Egdon Heath. Then, when they are married and Eustacia has at last begun to understand that Clym is not going to fulfil her ambitions, she regrets her decision to jilt Damon and, indeed, meets her death trying to run away with him.

This dance of characters, this neat plotting, is carefully organised with reference to place. The characters travel a great deal and, as we saw in Chapter 2, the settings are chosen to reflect the different phases of their development. That very word 'phase' is, of course, the title Hardy gives to the different sections of *Tess of the d'Urbervilles*. The travelling in itself creates a structure and, although it is a technique of Hardy's that is not often discussed, it is worth looking at in detail. It works very well because the reader easily and automatically accepts the events that take place in the different settings precisely because those settings create the right atmosphere for the events. The classic example here is *Tess of the d'Urbervilles* where Tess's long dance with Angel and Alec takes place over a large area of South Wessex and ranges from the poverty of Marlott to the elegance of Sandbourne and from the lush meadows of Talbothays to the frozen fields of Flintcomb-Ash.

So the novels are carefully constructed as to plots and settings, organised into coherent patterns which can be reduced to diagrams to emphasise their simplicity and neatness. This can be a useful exercise when you are first studying Hardy and although, of course, it leaves out a great deal, drawing a diagram can help you to understand structure. Here are some examples:

(1) Bathsheba Everdene at the centre of the triangle of forces in *Far From The Madding Crowd*
(2) Henchard and Farfrae reversing roles in *The Mayor of Casterbridge*
(3) Tess's wanderings in *Tess of the d'Urbervilles*
(4) Sue and Jude's travels in *Jude the Obscure*

In addition to these structures of plot and place Hardy organises his fiction by a judicious use of symbolism. He pursues certain symbols or metaphors in such a way that they, too, form a pattern, a structure that holds the novels together. An obvious example is the broad metaphor of the cycle of the seasons which is several times repeated. It is strongly marked in *Far From the Madding Crowd* where the different stages of the novel are firmly set against the background of the farming year and Hardy is able to make much of the symbolic significance of each season as it passes. Thus when Boldwood first courts Bathsheba it is during the summer and we see her in the June heat surrounded by the oppressive weight of his hot and passionate feeling for her. Less warm occasions, such as the death of Fanny Robin, the shooting of Troy and the quiet marriage of Bathsheba and Gabriel take place at more appropriate times of year – at midwinter or in rainy weather.

In *Tess of the d'Urbervilles* this same seasonal symbolism appears again. Tess is raped (or seduced) on an autumn night, at perhaps the earliest time of the year when a field might be ploughed, and she has her baby in the summer, during the harvest. As in the previous example, Hardy is using these symbolic connexions to underline man's inextricable involvement with nature but also to carry on the structure or pattern of his dance. Thus it comes to us as no surprise that it is in the following spring that Tess's spirits start to revive and she begins again to think what she will make of her life.

Besides these seasonal symbols, Hardy carefully associates his characters with patterns of allusion of other kinds. In *The Woodlanders*, for instance, Giles Winterborne is a tree-planter and, later, an itinerant cider-maker. In the first capacity we see him possessed of 'an extraordinary power of making trees grow' and he is deeply associated with the long-term, positive, faithful connotations of his occupation. (Fitzpiers, conversely, is associated with the cutting-down of a tree.) Then, in his later incarnation, we see Giles involved in the more ephemeral occupation of pressing the products of trees (apples) into cider and we realise at once that he has been uprooted. Equally, in the cider-pressing scene he is described as looking like 'Autumn's very brother' which makes us at once think of his name – Winterborne. Then, when he dies during the winter we begin to see that he, too, has been associated with a seasonal pattern – only in his case it has all been winter (when tree-planting occurs) or autumn and never spring or summer. This symbolises his bad luck and his thwarted love for Grace Melbury.

Hardy's patterns of symbolism, once noticed, are fairly easy to interpret. When Tess is marked out with a red head-band in the opening phase of the novel, and when, later she is splashed with Prince's blood and pricked by Alec's present of roses we begin to see that she is being prepared as the sacrificial victim. Then when she is so often compared to various harmless animals and, particularly, to birds, we begin to think of her as trapped, in the power of man, likely to be slaughtered. With one of the great Hardy novels, such as *Tess of the d'Urbervilles,* it is in fact possible to attribute some symbolic or metaphorical value to almost the whole of the text so that it would be inappropriate to see the symbols as some sort of decoration; they are a major technique which Hardy uses to give body to his plots. The success of his novels may have much to do with the fact that he integrates plot, setting and symbol into a coherent and unified structure where there is nothing out of place and no random or unexplained element.

This tight structure is, of course, conventional in many eighteenth- and nineteenth-century novels. From Henry Fielding's (1707-54) *Tom Jones* (1749), which Coleridge considered to be the best-plotted novel he knew, through Jane Austen (1775-1817), in whose novels there is never a word out of place, to the work of George Eliot (1819-90) the tradition is clear. Admittedly the effervescent genius of Dickens created novels which have been called 'great baggy monsters', and there are times when a reader may wonder in the middle of *Bleak House* (1852-53) or *Our Mutual Friend* (1864-65) quite what has happened to many of the characters and elements of plot that have been introduced so far. But even Dickens chooses, like Thackeray and Trollope (1815-82), to draw all the threads together at the end, to *close* his novels as completely as he can, and certainly the overwhelming tendency in the English novel of the nineteenth century is towards exactly the sort of tight structure we have been examining in Hardy.

It might be useful, indeed, to see Hardy's structures as being hyper-conventional. That is, he takes the need for a coherent plot and a thorough ending to an extreme. His novels *close* very definitely and unambiguously, the dance is completed. Whereas Dickens or George

Eliot might employ a symbol here or there, or make an association that recurs, Hardy is almost relentless in his pursuit of a symbolic pattern. Thus in one way he stands at the end of a particular novelistic tradition. In the hands of his contemporary, Henry James (1843-1916), and in the hands of immediate successors such as Joseph Conrad (1857-1924), this tradition has been greatly modified, and it has gone on changing ever since. Hardy, who had so many new, shocking and unconventional things to say chose, wisely perhaps, to express them in traditional, even hyper-conventional, structures.

Style

It is tempting to assume that Hardy, the countryman, must somehow write in a fresh, natural, simple style, but this assumption would certainly be wrong. He did not, of course, write in a grotesque or mannered or unnatural style – indeed he often has a devastating honesty and directness about him. But there is nothing of the Wordsworthian rustic about him, much less the country bumpkin. His style is, on the whole, educated, objective, controlled and largely formal. He does not indulge in many impassioned outbursts or flights of rhetoric and, just as he is never merely simple or naïve, so he is never elaborate or ambiguous. He has a measured and steady style which preserves a certain formality which often passes unnoticed. And yet, breaking through this surface time and again, Hardy's characteristic voice subtly jars the harmony, surprises the reader by reminding him that all is not well, that this is not the world of Jane Austen any more.

In discussing the major novels, below, we shall be looking at certain passages from the point of view of their style, among other things, so for the moment some characteristic paragraphs from the minor fiction will be selected upon which we can concentrate.

First, from the point of view of the educated formality of Hardy's style, we can consider the following from the opening of *The Well-Beloved*. The first chapter of this novel is entitled 'A Supposititious Presentment of Her' and it begins thus:

A person who differed from the local wayfarers was climbing the steep road which leads through the sea-skirted townlet definable as the Street of Wells, and forms a pass into that Gibraltar of Wessex, the singular penninsula once an island, and still called such, that stretches out like the head of a bird into the English Channel. It is connected with the mainland by a long thin neck of pebbles 'cast up by the rages of the se', and unparalleled in its kind in Europe.

(*The Well-Beloved*, Chapter 1)

This is a conventional opening, formal enough. It introduces a person and a place with considerable economy and there is a feeling that a good deal of information has been packed into two sentences. Rather typically Hardy shows us a lone figure on a road, a favourite device of his, and he coins a word ('townlet') that reminds us of the coinages common in his poetry ('I'd have my life *unbe*' for instance, from 'Tess's Lament'). But although these and other details would mark this paragraph unmistakably as being by Hardy, it preserves a tone of measured objectivity, of logic, that is entirely conventional. The man is on the road, the road leads through a village, the village is named thus, it is on the way to such a place, this place has such-and-such geographical characteristics. Hardy even pauses to emphasise his objectivity by comparing the penninsula to Gibraltar, by hinting at some historical research he has done (whence, presumably, the archaic spelling 'se' for 'sea') and by pointing out that the 'neck of pebbles' is unique in Europe. The urbane, travelled, well-read author settles down to tell us a tale.

More formal yet is this paragraph from *Two on a Tower* in which Hardy describes the effect on the astronomer Swithin St. Cleeve and Lady Constantine of their secret marriage.

> Perhaps the most remarkable feature in their exploit was its comparative effectiveness as an expedient for the end design, – that of restoring calm assiduity to the study of astronomy. Swithin took up his old position as the lonely philosopher at the column, and Lady Constantine lapsed back to immured existence at the house, with apparently not a friend in the parish. The enforced narrowness of life which her limited resources necessitated was now an additional safeguard against the discovery of her relations with St. Cleeve. Her neighbours seldom troubled her; as much, it must be owned, from a tacit understanding that she was not in a position to return invitations as from any selfish coldness engendered by her want of wealth.
>
> (*Two on a Tower*, Chapter 21)

What at once strikes us here is the rather heavy Latinate vocabulary and the slightly antique quality of the writing. Although written in 1882 these sentences might just conceivably have been written in 1782, and certainly they could have been written during the first half of the nineteenth century. 'Expedient for the end design', 'calm assiduity', 'immured existence', 'enforced narrowness' and words such as 'necessitated' and 'engendered' have about them that slight opacity, that need for simultaneous translation as it were, of eighteenth-century prose. 'Immured' means walled-in, 'narrowness' means poverty, and so on. We even find ourselves wondering if 'discovery' is being used in its modern sense of 'being found out' or in the sense in which Henry Fielding and Jane Austen use it to mean 'revelation'.

This formal prose is precise and controlled. It gives us exactly the picture that the author wishes to paint. It links the more dramatic episodes very well and engenders in us a sense of Hardy's balance and judgement. We feel we are in good hands when we hear our narrator employing in the last sentence one of the old classical figures of speech that offer a fair-sounding balance such as 'as much from . . . as from'. There, we notice that the alternatives are even given the same number of words: we can balance one neighbour's generous 'she was not in a position to return invitations' with another neighbour's view encapsulated in the words 'any selfish coldness engendered by her want of wealth'. The writer must be a man of experience, a sane and sensible fellow; this narrator we can rely on, he has no prejudices.

Or so it seems; for Hardy, of course, has a passionately committed view of the universe, and his style, carefully scrutinised, reveals this, too. Just as *The Well-Beloved* opens with the revealing image of a solitary man toiling up a road in a rocky country (where, soon, he will meet a woman) in such a way that we find we are being pulled in one particular direction by the undertow of the prose, so the opening of *Two on a Tower*, formal as it is, gives away a little of Hardy's game.

On an early winter afternoon, clear but not cold, when the vegetable world was a weird multitude of skeletons through whose ribs the sun shone freely, a gleaming landau came to pause on the crest of a hill in Wessex. The spot was where the old Melchester Road, which the carriage had hitherto followed, was joined by a drive that led round into a park at no great distance off.

(*Two on a Tower*, Chapter 1)

Here again we have people (in the carriage presumably) and place and plenty of information in a small space. Stylistically this is a conventional opening, setting time and place before us and describing the winter's day rather well. But there is something unsettling in the metaphor Hardy chooses to convey the impression of the trees and shrubs; of course, these are leafless, or in the well-worn metaphor, 'bare', but Hardy goes further than that. For him they are 'skeletons' with 'ribs' who stand in a 'weird' group. This subversive element is utterly typical of Hardy: the sentences seem conventional, unambiguous, calm, objective and controlled. And so they are, except for the skeletons that pop out at us and then vanish, for a time.

This somewhat formal style, with its occasional subversive elements, is, then, characteristic of Hardy's fiction. Sometimes he raises the tone to the pitch of an Old Testament prophet, as in the opening chapter of *The Return of the Native*, where Egdon Heath is so magnificently described, and sometimes he lowers it to passages of homely description, particularly in such novels as *The Trumpet-Major*, with its descriptions of Overcombe Mill, and *Under the Greenwood Tree*, with its abundance of detail about the Dewy household. But he always affects a certain detachment and an educated tone. His comparisons are often with paintings, or with elements from classical literature, or with biblical characters, rather than with natural phenomena. Although he is the great painter of Wessex scenery his fiction in the end belongs to the head, it is a cerebral business just as much as the fiction of a George Eliot or a Henry James.

There is one exception to this, and it is to do with dialogue. Readers of *Under the Greenwood Tree*, for example, may well be surprised at Hardy's style being called formal. That would be because that novel abounds in dialogue and Hardy, naturally enough, imitates the style of the speakers in his passages of dialogue. The more educated characters are inclined to speak quite formally; prigs such as Henry Knight in *A Pair of Blue Eyes* often speak as though they were reading a speech, although of course this is a deliberate device to make Knight seem pompous in contrast with the fresh and youthful Stephen. The less well-educated characters, however, show how good Hardy's ear was for another kind of English altogether. In *Under the Greenwood Tree*, for example, tranter Dewy is talking to his rustic cronies about the fact that his son's new bride has admitted that when she says it takes 'only a minute' to put on her bonnet she really means five minutes.

> 'Ah, sonnies!' said the tranter . . . ''tis a talent of the female race that low numbers should stand for high, more especially in matters of waiting, matters of age and matters of money.' 'True, true, upon my body,' said Geoffrey. 'Ye spak with feeling, Geoffrey, seemingly.' 'Anybody that d'know my experience might guess that.'

Tranter Dewy then asks Geoffrey about his wife, who has not attended the wedding:

> 'What's she doing now, Geoffrey?'
> 'Claning out all the upstairs drawers and cupboards, and dusting all the second-best chainey – a thing that's only done once a year. "If there's work to be done I must do it," she says, "wedding or no." '
> ''Tis my belief she's a very good woman at bottom.'
> 'She's terrible deep, then.'
> Mrs. Penny turned round. 'Well, 'tis humps and hollers with the best of us . . .'
> (*Under the Greenwood Tree*, Part 5, Chapter 2)

In this sort of an exchange we hear an entirely different voice that Hardy can employ. He lightly touches in the Dorset accent ('spak', 'claning') and some of the Dorset turns of phrase ('the female race') in a way which indicates his deep familiarity with the obviously somewhat jocular nature of Wessex speech. These sections of dialogue contain most of the humour in Hardy's novels, and the country people who participate in them have a significant normalising and humanising role to play. They have been designated Hardy's 'rustic chorus' and Hardy keeps them at a humble level where they neither achieve greatness nor run the risks of a tragic fate. *Under the Greenwood Tree* is almost entirely devoted to the doings of one such 'chorus'. Dick and Fancy, the hero and heroine, are set a little apart from them but there is as yet no deep division between the different levels of the novel. In *Far From the Madding Crowd* the rustic chorus is important but it is distinctly only a background, and in the later novels the whole choric element is gradually dropped, although it does not disappear entirely and its last appearance is perhaps in Widow Edlin at the end of *Jude the Obscure*.

Dialogue, then, enables Hardy to adopt different styles, especially the rustic style, and to contrast this with the educated style of his normal narration.

Hardy's narrative

Hardy narrates his stories in the third person, as a traditional omniscient narrator. As in the case of the structure and the style of his novels, he adopts largely conventional narrative approaches. Generally speaking, little of importance has happened before the narrator takes up the story. There is *some* past, of course, but it tends to be neutral and not of great importance; certainly Hardy does not employ the 'flashback' technique very much. If we try to think of things that happened 'before' the start of any of the novels the list is not very long: Clym Yeobright's Parisian experience (in *The Return of the Native*) and Mrs Charmond's earlier meeting with Fitzpiers (in *The Woodlanders*) are two examples, and they are not major events. When Hardy wants to insert an early or preliminary scene he simply does so at the beginning of the novel: in *The Mayor of Casterbridge*, for example, the wife-selling incident, instead of being saved up, as it might have been by Dickens, for the *dénouement*, is simply put in its proper place – right at the beginning of the story which it initiated. Similarly, in *Far From the Madding Crowd*, Oak's early interest in Bathsheba, and his original status as 'Farmer Oak' are boldly and directly explained in the first chapter. There is thus no element of detective work, at least in Hardy's major novels. He begins at the beginning, goes on to the end, then stops.

This omniscient and straightforward narrator does not stay entirely aloof from his narrative. From time to time he introduces a comment on the action and this helps us to understand what is going on and to stand back from it a little. His comments vary from almost unnoticeable asides to some obtrusive and highly significant observations.

In the first category we have this description of Elfride Swancourt. At the end of a sentence about her perversity in feeling obliged to meet a man she no longer loves Hardy adds: 'For she was markedly one of those who sigh for the unattainable – to whom superlatively, a hope is pleasing because not a possession' (*A Pair of Blue Eyes*, Chapter 20).

This is typical of Hardy in that it is not left to apply to Elfride only but is instead elevated to the status of a general moral comment about a whole section of humanity 'those . . . to whom'. This is Hardy the psychologist at work alongside the action of his novel, as it were; the narrator draws conclusions from his narration. A more extended example comes from *Two on a Tower*. Here the narrator is explaining what it is that may attract Bishop Helmsdale to Lady Constantine.

> A bachelor, he rejoiced in the commanding period of life that stretches between the time of waning impulse and the time of incipient dotage, when a woman can reach the male heart neither by awakening a young man's passion nor an old man's infatuation. He must be made to admire or he can be made to do nothing.
>
> (*Two on a Tower*, Chapter 25)

Nothing more is said about this, it is almost a mere aside, a generalisation of the narrator's. It has the effect of making us think of more men than just the Bishop, and we automatically think of ourselves and of our friends to test whether the generalisation is true. This sort of interjection stops the flow of narrative but it keeps us at a suitable distance from the events that are taking place and enables us to judge them better.

In the second category, of more significant asides by the narrator, we have an example in the remarkable paragraph that concludes Chapter 14 of *Tess of the d'Urbervilles*. Here Tess's baby Sorrow is buried in the churchyard at Marlott.

> So the baby was . . . buried by lanternlight . . . in that shabby corner of God's allotment where He lets the nettles grow, and where all unbaptized infants, notorious drunkards, suicides and other of the conjecturally damned are laid.
>
> (*Tess of the d'Urbervilles*, Chapter 14)

Hardy is sometimes accused of being unsubtle, of making his point too forcibly, but here is an example of his ironic and somewhat veiled style in a pregnant aside. The passage turns, probably, on the word 'conjecturally' and from that, and from the faintly sardonic 'God's allotment', as well as from the bizarre yoking together of suicides, drunks and infants, we gain an impression of veiled, even humorous criticism. The narrator himself has never damned anyone, in this novel or elsewhere, and indeed at the end of the scene in the Chase where Tess and Alec first make love he has specifically repudiated divine justice. So we pick up the tone of this aside easily enough and quickly perceive something pagan, fatalistic and atheistic behind it. It is with such interventions as these that Hardy affirms his control over the reader; setting, structure, style and symbolism all add up to a fully coherent and unambiguous statement (it is significant that there are no widely divergent interpretations of Hardy, there is hardly room for them) and this is underpinned by authorial intrusions which keep us from wandering from the course we are destined to follow.

Chapter 4

'Novels of Character and Environment'

NOTE: In this and the following chapters each of Hardy's works will be considered in turn, keeping to his own categories as far as the fiction is concerned (see pp. 13-14, above), and dealing with his poetry and *The Dynasts* in a separate chapter. For each novel there is a summary of the plot, a general commentary, and a brief list of points that will help further study.

Tess of the d'Urbervilles (1891)

The plot

Jack Durbeyfield, an itinerant dealer in farm produce, living at Marlott in South Wessex is informed that he is probably a descendant of the ancient d'Urberville family who were given land in Wessex by William the Conqueror. He is amazed and the information disturbs his humble life. His daughter, Tess, the mainstay of his somewhat feckless household, meets a young man, Angel Clare, the son of a clergyman, at a country dance. Later, driving the family cart, Tess has an accident and their horse is killed. Feeling guilty at having thus deprived the family of its livelihood, Tess accepts her mother's suggestion that she should visit a nearby rich family, who call themselves d'Urberville, and 'claim kin', that is, ask for their help on the grounds of blood relationship.

Tess's visit is in some ways a success. She makes a good impression on the d'Urberville household and is·offered work. The son of the house, Alec, however, is attracted to her, pays attentions to her and eventually takes advantage of her tiredness late one night and either rapes or seduces her. Tess returns home to Marlott and discovers that she is pregnant. She gives birth to a baby who soon dies.

Two years later Tess leaves home again and walks to Talbothays farm where she is employed as a darymaid and where she meets Angel Clare again. Gradually, in spite of the difference in their social positions, Angel falls in love with her and she with him. She tries to resist his proposals of marriage and tries to warn him that she is a 'fallen' woman, but she fails and they are finally married. On their wedding night Angel confesses to an earlier affair he had had with a woman in London. Tess, encouraged by this, confesses her entanglement with Alec. Angel is shocked and, after a nocturnal struggle with himself, abandons Tess and goes, eventually, to Brazil.

Tess is left to fend for herself and finds work on a farm a lot less comfortable than Talbothays, called Flintcomb-Ash, where the work is hard and the weather bitter. She considers appealing to Angel's parents for help but is unable to do so. Then she meets Alec d'Urberville again. At first it seems that he has reformed and is now an itinerant preacher, but his old attraction to Tess is strong and he soon gives up his preaching and again makes approaches to her. She resists but it becomes apparent that Alec is helping her family, who have become destitute and, in spite of an impassioned letter to Angel to come and rescue her, she at last gives in to Alec again and becomes his mistress; they go and live together at the seaside resort of Sandbourne.

Angel, much more thoughtful after various trials and tribulations in Brazil, returns and seeks Tess. When he finds her she is horrified at what she has done, impulsively murders Alec and leaves Sandbourne with Angel. They spend a belated honeymoon together in a deserted house and Tess is finally caught by the police at Stonehenge. She is hanged and Angel walks off with Tess's younger sister, 'Liza-'Lu.

Commentary

Tess is often considered to be Hardy's greatest novel. He himself evidently thought so, which may be the reason why he put it at the head of his list of his most serious novels. It is apparent from the biographies that he was much moved by the stage version of the novel and that he thought of his heroine almost as though she were a real person.

The power of the novel comes from a number of sources. First, here Hardy creates his best and most thoroughly realised heroine. It is as if he has learnt from the creation of all his previous heroines and has finally achieved the depiction of a woman who is not to be satirised or patronised and who is not limited or pathetic. Fancy Day, in *Under the Greenwood Tree*, is a lightweight, almost a flirt; Bathsheba Everdene, in *Far From the Madding Crowd*, is presented to us in terms of that most 'feminine' of failings – vanity – and although she grows in stature as the novel progresses we are always watching her progress from above, as it were, with something of a satirical eye on her shortcomings. Fanny Robin, in the same novel, has a tragic fate (and a baby) like Tess, but she is a poor, weak, pathetic creature. Eustacia Vye, in *The Return of the Native*, has Tess's passion and emotional power but she is unstable, unsure of herself, wayward. Elizabeth-Jane Henchard, in *The Mayor of Casterbridge*, has got the measure of life but she is a quiet, steady, homely body, who cannot rise to tragic status. The list could go on. Tess alone, however, is passionate and intelligent and powerful and humane and without any supposed feminine weaknesses. We do not see *her* from 'above' or with a satirical eye.

Hardy achieves something extraordinary in his creation of this heroine. She comes from a comic-rustic background, she is a mere milkmaid, she has an illegitimate child largely because of her simple ignorance of men. And yet, even allowing for the greater class-consciousness of the 1890s, we are never tempted to laugh at her or to patronise her. She is always dignified, complete, sensual, honest, true, whether she is baptising her dying infant or laughing with her fellow dairymaids at Talbothays. Hardy was evidently a feminist, always at least as interested in his female characters as in his male characters, but only in the person of Tess does he fully bring off the portrayal of a complete woman. Ironically, perhaps, the heroine nearest to Tess in character is Ethelberta Chickerel in *The Hand of Ethelberta*. She takes charge of her younger brothers and sisters, as Tess does, and contrives to manage her own life through a careful use of her attributes of beauty and intelligence, but this novel, as we shall see when we discuss it below, is a satire on London society and various sorts and conditions of men so that, although it has a love interest, it does not pretend to be fully serious in the way *Tess* is.

The second source of the power of *Tess* lies in its rich evocation of Wessex, its landscape and the old way of life there. The novel dwells on the Vale of Blackmoor and when we first see this stretch of country, with the attenuated May-day dance taking place, something of a pastoral idyll is presented to us. Subsequent scenes take this further – Tess suckling her baby in the cornfield during harvest, and all the many scenes at Talbothays dairy. The other side of the coin is represented by the d'Urberville's house, for instance:

> Everything in this snug property was bright, thriving, and well kept; acres of glass-houses stretched down the inclines to the copses at their feet. Everything looked like money – like the last coin issued from the Mint.

(*Tess of the d'Urbervilles*, Chapter 5)

This stands in deliberate contrast with the Durbeyfields' cottage tucked away in the muddy but beautiful Blackmoor vale – the only 'acres' that d'Urberville seems to possess are made of glass, everything is shiny and new.

The old world, or real acres of meadow and pasture, is evoked best at Talbothays, a farm in a region where, Hardy says, Tess 'felt akin to the landscape'. The descriptions of the farm work here, of Tess, Angel and the others carefully combing a field of rich grass to find the few garlic plants that are spoiling the butter, or of their going out in the early morning mist to milk the cows, are beautifully done and serve to keep the characters' feet firmly planted in the Wessex soil. Man and nature are so closely associated as to seem inseparable and this makes us continually refer back to nature when we judge Tess and the others. Is Alec's action in raping her 'natural' or not? Is the birth of her illegitimate baby 'natural'? Is Angel's reaction when he hears of this baby 'natural'? The characters are so closely identified with nature that these questions are forced upon us – as are the answers to them.

The third source of the power of *Tess* is its allegorical element. We know we are reading a novel about a heroine who fascinates and impresses us, we know that we are reading about Wessex and its landscape and its old ways, but we also know that we are being asked to consider the whole matter of mankind's fate and its relationship with the universe. The novel is a tragedy – things tend to go badly, it seems – but why is this? Of course, human institutions are imperfect, society hypocritical and harsh, education inadequate, but *Tess* seems to rise above these levels and question the whole universal system and what it does to man. Early in the novel, when Tess and her brother Abraham are driving the horse and cart on its fatal journey, Abraham asks Tess if the stars are worlds. She says 'Yes' and he continues.

> 'All like ours?'
> 'I don't know; but I think so. They sometimes seem to be like the apples on our stubbard-tree. Most of them splendid and sound – a few blighted.'
> 'Which do we live on – a splendid one or a blighted one?'
> 'A blighted one'.
>
> (*Tess of the d'Urbervilles*, Chapter 4)

This, and other similar reflections by the characters, or by Hardy himself in his authorial intrusions, sets the key for the novel, as it were. We are always aware of deeper meanings and suggestions below the surface of the text. Angel, for instance, is an angel, complete with harp, and we are asked, surely, to consider whether he behaves angelically: as a sort of avenging angel of the Old Testament kind he may be punishing Tess for her supposed sin, but as a more human and perhaps Christian angel should he not forgive her and support her rather than abandon her? Tess herself is the 'Maiden' who is seduced by the 'Devil' (Alec is constantly associated with faintly infernal ideas, objects and colours – pitchforks, smoke, redness) and the result of their union, of course, is 'Sorrow'.

In addition to these three aspects there are several others. *Tess* is, for instance, a novel about nineteenth-century society, and points a finger at the damage that certain sorts of class division can do (this is not so much an attack on snobbery as a warning about the difficulties inherent in a marriage between a vicar's son and a milkmaid) and at the double standard of the time whereby sexual experience could be seen as less reprehensible in a man before marriage than in a woman.

Tess is also a funny novel, which may be surprising but only goes to indicate the complexity of Hardy's genius. The 'rustic chorus', of course, provides most of the humour: the villagers in Marlott and the dairymaids at Talbothays, led by their employer, Farmer Crick, have moments where they are most amusing. Hardy even manages an ironical tone from time to time in his most tragic passages – in his commentary on the rape scene, for instance, and in his description of the corner of the graveyard where Sorrow is buried.

Points for study

---

1. *The presentation of Tess herself*
Hardy presents Tess with extreme care. Look closely at the words he uses to describe her in the first 'phase': she is made to seem very young (innocence), she has large eyes (sensitivity), she is 'modest . . . expressive . . . soft' she wears a 'thin white gown' (purity and fragility) and we see her standing alone. Then we begin to notice a pattern of association between Tess and the colour red: she alone of the girls at the 'club-walking' has a red band to mark her out; she is splashed by the horse's blood at the time of the cart accident; she pricks herself on the roses given to her by Alec (tragic victim). Later in the novel she is associated with birds, flies, cows, certain landscapes. Hardy controls the reader's reactions to Tess very carefully: watch what he is doing.

2. *The use of seasons*
Like *Far From the Madding Crowd*, *Tess* is based in part on the pathetic fallacy of attributing to nature a sympathy with human emotions. That is to say, Tess's fortunes bear some relationship to the time of year in which they take place so that weather and other conditions offer some commentary on what is taking place. You can trace this pattern for yourself, but as reference points you might take: May-day, when Angel and Tess first meet; the summer, during which both the corn and Tess's baby come to fruition; the spring when her spirits revive; the summer of Angel's hot courtship, and so on.

3. *'A pure woman'*
The subtitle of the novel offers a challenge. It asks us to consider Tess and the other characters from a *moral* point of view. Is she pure? Is Angel? Is Alec impure? Are Marian, the dairymaid at Talbothays, and

Izz Huett, impure in their very natural desire for Angel Clare? Is Tess impure when she returns to Alec at the end of the novel? Her motives, even then, are a compound of desperation and a desire to help her family – does that justify becoming a man's mistress?

4. *The rape*

Hardy offers several explanations, in his discussion of the 'rape' (it is not clear that there is any violence involved, whence the inverted commas) and they are worth considering in detail. The section concerned consists of the last four paragraphs of Chapter 11, the end of the first 'Phase' of Tess's story. Hardy is at pains to associate the event, and Tess herself in particular, with nature ('gentle roosting birds', 'hopping rabbits and hares') but he adopts a very educated and sophisticated tone in which to discuss the social and psychological damage which is being done. He suggests that the blame for this is perhaps to be attributed to Tess's guardian angel or to her God, and he suggests that there may be some question of retribution for the behaviour of Tess's 'mailed ancestors'. But really he is just puzzled, simply at a loss to explain the disparity between what happens to Tess and what we feel *ought* to happen to her. He almost shrugs his shoulders when he says 'many thousand years of analytic philosophy have failed to explain' this sort of disaster to our 'sense of order'.

5. *The web*

Tess seems fated, caught up in the web of circumstances that lead to her doom. This is not a matter of bad luck or random chance: there is an iron logic in the development of people's fates. It is because Tess is the prettiest and most intelligent of her children that her mother sends her to 'claim kin' with Alec, and it is precisely these same qualities that lead Alec to fall in love with her, to deflower her, to pursue her. Then again these very same qualities are what marks her out for the interest of Angel Clare and are, ironically, what make him so sure that she is a 'pure' woman. The web starts to be woven when Parson Tringham drops his casual word to Jack Durbeyfield in the opening scene of the novel. It is a worthwhile exercise to analyse how Hardy follows this thread and, matching it with others, weaves the net in which Tess is so inexorably caught.

6. *The loss of faith*

The universal significance of the novel is emphasised by Hardy's minor theme of the loss of religious faith. Hidden inside the main story is another one. Angel Clare, we see at once, is not as religious as his brothers, who are made to seem somewhat priggish and bigoted. He is able to shake off his father's rather narrow Christianity in the same way as he is able to break social conventions and marry a dairymaid. When he returns from Brazil we discover that he is more or less an agnostic and that he certainly does not believe in life after death. But it is obvious that he has held agnostic opinions earlier, too, in the days of his happiness: he as much as says so to his father and, more significantly, Tess is able to relay Angel's 'negations' to Alec once the latter has turned preacher. In this minor story Angel 'deconverts' Tess who 'deconverts' Alec. Ironically, of course, this very deconversion is one of the reasons why Alec and Tess resume their affair at the end of the novel. Besides this, the vicar with whom Tess discusses Sorrow's baptism (Chapter 14) is specifically portrayed as a sceptic.

Far From the Madding Crowd (1874)

The plot

Gabriel Oak, a small farmer in South Wessex, meets by chance a 'wild' young girl, Bathsheba Everdene, falls in love with her and after some further meetings offers to marry her. She refuses him, because she does not love him, and leaves the district to go to Weatherbury. Oak encounters a misfortune in which his entire flock of sheep is destroyed and he has to start again in life. He has no luck in obtaining work until he arrives at Weatherbury where a fortuitous opportunity to help to put out a burning straw-rick on a farm brings him face to face with Bathsheba again. It turns out to be *her* farm, which she has inherited from her uncle, and she takes Oak on, at his suggestion, as a shepherd.

Oak falls in with the Weatherbury farm-workers, Joseph Poorgrass, Jan Coggan, Henery Fraye and the others, and we meanwhile discover that Fanny Robin, a servant at Bathsheba's farm, has run away in pursuit of a soldier in the nearby town of Casterbridge who has promised to marry her. We are also introduced to a stern bachelor neighbour of Bathsheba's – Farmer Boldwood. As a joke, Bathsheba sends Boldwood a Valentine card saying 'Marry Me'. The joke misfires because Boldwood falls suddenly and violently in love with her. Meanwhile Fanny Robin does arrange to marry her soldier, Sergeant Troy, but she goes to the wrong church in Casterbridge; Troy, who feels he has been made a fool of, refuses to set another date for their wedding.

Boldwood courts Bathsheba who refuses his offer of marriage but Oak suffers as he sees them together and he even leaves Bathsheba's employment for a while. An emergency on the farm, however, when her sheep become ill and only Oak can cure them, brings him back when Bathsheba pleads with him to return. Then Sergeant Troy, who is a native of Weatherbury, meets Bathsheba by chance when he is back in the village on a visit. She falls in love with him, seeing him as romantic and glamorous, and they are secretly married in Bath, to the fury and despair of Boldwood.

Troy is a poor husband and a poor farmer. Were it not for Oak's care and attention, Bathsheba's farm would go to rack and ruin. Troy spends her money gambling and drinking and soon neglects her. Meanwhile Fanny Robin, consumptive, abandoned and pregnant, crawls into the Casterbridge workhouse and dies. Her body is brought to Weatherbury and into Bathsheba's house where it is found by Troy whose old love for Fanny rekindles; after a scene with Bathsheba in which he says that he has always preferred Fanny to her, he leaves her. He stays long enough to plant flowers on Fanny's grave, but when these are washed away by the rain he abandons Weatherbury and wanders down to the seaside where he goes for a swim, is swept out by the current and rescued by some sailors with whom he sails away.

Bathsheba is now left in an ambiguous position. If Troy is dead but his body is not found she may remarry after seven years; Boldwood forces her to promise to marry him at the end of that time. Oak is made bailiff on the farm. Troy reappears briefly, but disguised and working in a travelling circus. He decides to reclaim his position as Bathsheba's husband by appearing at the very Christmas eve party at which she will have to give her promise to marry Boldwood. When all the guests are assembled he appears and claims her. Boldwood, utterly distracted, shoots him and gives himself up at the local gaol. A petition saves him from execution, but he is given a long term of imprisonment. Bathsheba gradually recovers and discovers that Oak has, after all, become indispensable to her and they are quietly married.

Commentary

Hardy told Leslie Stephen that while writing *Far From the Madding Crowd* he was living 'within a walk of the district within which the incidents are supposed to occur. I find it a great advantage to be actually among the people described at the time of describing them'. This fits well with the reader's impression of the novel: it is full of agricultural and rustic detail that was evidently gathered by an expert, and a native, at the time of writing. More than any of his other novels, more even than *Tess*, *Far From the Madding Crowd* is a celebration of the old ways of life in Wessex and its action is inextricably bound up with the seasons and the work and difficulties which they bring to a farm in their passing. This was Hardy's home territory. Outside the towns, life even in modern Dorset villages is noticeably agricultural; in Hardy's day the integration of man, work, landscape and season was still almost complete.

The names of the characters hint at this: Gabriel Oak is a sturdy English tree, Fanny Robin a small, delicate and bird-like creature, Joseph Poorgrass is not the most advanced or successful of individuals. (Boldwood seems to be a name that points to the Middle-English word 'wood' or 'wode' meaning 'mad' rather than to a forest.) The incidents of the novel are all made to the pattern of the agricultural year. Bathsheba rescues Gabriel from possible suffocation in his hut at midwinter lambing time; Gabriel is ruined in the ensuing month in time to offer himself at the hiring fair for spring and summer work; as the season progresses Boldwood proposes to Bathsheba at the sheep-washing (sheep-dipping we would call it now) and Bathsheba discusses her position with Gabriel while he is sharpening the shears to use on the sheep; during the shearing itself Gabriel sees Bathsheba with Boldwood and he quarrels with her; then, at the time when clover is ripest in the midsummer, her sheep stray into the clover field, fall sick, and Gabriel has to rescue them; Troy makes his approaches to Bathsheba during the summer, too, conveniently looking glamorous in his soldier's uniform while he helps the rustics with the hay-making; they are married in the summer; their marriage begins to break up in the autumn and Fanny dies then; it is during autumn storms that the 'gurgoyle' undoes Troy's work on Fanny's grave; the climax of the novel is held over from that winter to the next, to allow for Bathsheba's supposed time of mourning, and occurs at Christmas, at midwinter again, so that the novel, except for the afterthought of Gabriel's marriage to Bathsheba, has come full circle.

Within this rustic framework Hardy deploys, in its most perfect form, a pattern that underlies many of his novels. It is a more complex version of the eternal triangle and usually consists of a woman surrounded by three suitors; the dilemma of this position is fundamentally the question of which one she loves but there are more superficial considerations, too, such as the expediency of marrying one rather than another. This pattern, which is clearly to be seen in *Under the Greenwood Tree* (Fancy Day – Dewy, Maybold, Shiner) and *The Hand of Ethelberta* (Ethelberta – Julian, Ladywell, Neigh, Mountclere) appears at its fullest and most convincing in *Far From the Madding Crowd*.

Hardy is a connoisseur of the emotion of love and the three men involved in this dance-like pattern have different ways of being in love and behave differently as a result. The woman at the centre of the dance is a psychological study, too, of course, and has her own ways of being or not being in love, so the interest is not merely in the pattern as a whole but in the individuals too. Thus, Gabriel is the quiet, steady, faithful lover who does not expect much in the way of return. He expresses his love by actions rather than words, notably actions such as saving hayricks from fire and rain, or saving sick sheep from death, which preserve not merely something of Bathsheba's but something which will be of benefit to the whole community. Hardy is in something of a dilemma about this himself, because he needs Gabriel to be hopelessly in love with Bathsheba (he was always fascinated by such torments, witness Giles Winterborne and Grace Melbury in *The Woodlanders*, for instance) but he also needs him to behave with the steadiness and devotion which are quite uncharacteristic of desperate love. He resolves this problem by inventing a new kind of love that is quite at variance with his assumptions elsewhere: a long-term, slow-growing affection that somehow gets people to love each other deeply without their both having 'fallen in love' first. This contradicts Hardy's general assumption that love cannot survive marriage, but it enables him to achieve some sort of balance at the end of this novel. Here is how he expresses it:

> Theirs was that substantial affection which arises . . . when the two who are thrown together begin first by knowing the rougher sides of each other's character, and not the best till further on, the romance growing up in the interstices of a mass of hard prosaic reality . . . the compounded feeling proves itself to be the only love which is strong as death – the love which many waters cannot quench, nor the floods drown, beside which the passion usually called by the name is evanescent as steam.

> (*Far From the Madding Crowd*, Chapter 56)

To make the point that there is something odd about this, the phrases in which Hardy points out the rarity of this emotion have been omitted. The last clause, however, even with these caveats, is clearly at variance with Hardy's opinion as stated or implied elsewhere.

Boldwood, more typically for Hardy, is the stern and reserved type, the strong character who, when once smitten with love, collapses completely. His farm goes to rack and ruin, his personality seems to be destroyed by the desperation of his passion, and he becomes a murderer. Such is the power of a force that, as we have just read, Hardy called 'evanescent as steam'. Troy is an odd mixture of different kinds of love. He provokes passion in Bathsheba (although she *claims* to have gone to Bath to finish with him she comes back married to him) and he seems interested in her at first although he soon tires of her. On the other hand his passion for Fanny Robin, which at first seems to be nothing at all as we watch her following him to Casterbridge, so pathetically anxious to marry him, proves to be extremely strong and saves him from the charge of being merely superficial, a trifler with the feelings of women.

Points for study

1. *The 'rustic chorus'*

Hardy's 'rustic chorus' – the group of minor characters who form a rich background to many of his novels and who comment on the action humorously but often shrewdly – is at its most developed in *Far From the Madding Crowd*. First, in this novel the 'chorus' is largest in number (with the possible exception of *The Return of the Native*); second, here it plays the largest part in the action; and, third, in this novel the hero most closely approximates to the status of a member of the group himself. Gabriel Oak is made of the same material as Joseph Poorgrass and the others; he may be a finer product but he has much in common with such people. In *Under the Greenwood Tree* many of the rustics belong to a category a little above that of mere farm labourer and perhaps Gabriel Oak is paralleled in this earlier novel by the men of the Dewy family who, as 'tranters' or carriers, are a cut above the farm workers. But Oak, the Dewys, and Hardy himself, know the language of these pleasant, ignorant near-peasants. In *Far From the Madding Crowd* Bathsheba, too, is of humble origins and has something in common with her work-folk.

The 'chorus' itself is present throughout the novel, often taking part in its most crucial episodes. Thus, for instance, Laban Tall, Henery Fraye, Joseph Poorgrass, Matthew Moon, William Smallbury and some others are all present at the scenes where Bathsheba receives a proposal from Boldwood (Chapter 19) and where she is forced to summon Gabriel's aid for her sick sheep (Chapter 21) and again it is Mark Clark and Jan Coggan who invite Joseph Poorgrass to drink with them at the Buck's Head when Joseph is bringing Fanny Robin's body back to Weatherbury from Casterbridge workhouse. This delay, represented in the novel by a touching and comic dialogue in the inn, brings about the necessity of leaving Fanny's body in Bathsheba's house overnight which in turn brings on all the ensuing dramatic events (Chapter 42). Similarly, the 'rustic chorus' has the last word in the novel, in reference to both Boldwood's reprieve from execution (Chapter 55) and the celebration of Gabriel's wedding to Bathsheba (Chapter 57).

2. *Spying*

Hardy has Gabriel Oak spy on, and watch over, Bathsheba a great deal in this novel. In the opening scene he is watching her from behind a hedge while she, thinking herself unobserved, indulges in the small vanity of looking at herself in a mirror (Chapter 1). In the next scene Gabriel spies on Bathsheba and her aunt through the cracks in a wooden shed where they are tending a sick cow in the middle of the night (Chapter 2). Then, immediately after this, we see Gabriel again watching Bathsheba while she performs some unusual actions on horseback (Chapter 3). This theme, which is repeated in various ways, such as Gabriel seeing Troy at Bathsheba's bedroom window one morning (Chapter 35), becomes more developed in later Hardy novels, and it seems to work in two ways. First it represents graphically the exclusion of the unsuccessful lover for whom there is always an obstacle barring his way to the beloved (witness Boldwood's cruel exclusion from Bathsheba's house by Troy in Chapter 34) and then it represents the power men can exert over women in Hardy, the secret control over other lives from a slight distance, and in this it is like the control exercised over Thomasin Yeobright by Diggory Venn in *The Return of the Native*.

3. *Balance of characters*
In the early novels (*Under the Greenwood Tree, Far From the Madding Crowd, The Return of the Native*) Hardy contrives to avoid concentration on one central character. Later, in *The Mayor of Casterbridge*, *Tess* and *Jude*, the central character becomes considerably more dominant. It is worth asking why this is so, and what is achieved by the more even-handed canvas painted in the early novels. It is tempting to say that Hardy is able to paint a better picture of country life by including a large number of characters and to explore the varieties of romantic love by having several main characters. But in *Tess* he seems to do both these things well enough. Might it be true that *Far From the Madding Crowd* is made up entirely of *equal* characters? Is Boldwood or Troy dealt with more sympathetically or in more detail than Fanny Robin or Joseph Poorgrass? Is Hardy attempting egalitarian fiction?

4. *Paper*
Hardy seems to be moving towards a type of fiction which, like Dickens's *Bleak House* (1853), is dominated by the written or spoken word, in particular by certain pieces of paper. Thus the Valentine that starts off the process of destruction in Boldwood is followed by the note that Bathsheba has to send Oak when her sheep are in trouble, by the note which Troy steals from Bathsheba in the refreshment tent, perhaps by the licence that Oak and Bathsheba need to get married at the end, and perhaps by Boldwood's written reprieve that is awaited so eagerly in Weatherbury. As for spoken words, there is much store set by Bathsheba on her aunt's having told Gabriel that she had many suitors when actually she had none, and by Boldwood on Bathsheba's promise to marry him and also by several other such people at crucial

moments. It is almost as if words had the power to dictate reality – but only almost.

Jude the Obscure (1895)

The plot

Jude Fawley, a small boy living with his aunt in the North Wessex village of Marygreen, impressed by the learning of his schoolmaster, Phillotson, decides to educate himself and if possible to go to study at Christminster (Oxford). After some difficulties he makes considerable progress in Latin, Greek and theology but an abrupt halt is put to this by Arabella, an attractive but uneducated village girl who seduces Jude and, by pretending to be pregnant, forces him to marry her. Their marriage is not successful and the divergence in their temperaments results in Arabella's departure for Australia with her family, who are emigrating.

Jude completes his apprenticeship as a stonemason and at last goes to Christminster to work there. He meets his cousin, Sue Bridehead, sensitive and somewhat wayward, and falls in love with her; but as a married man he cannot, of course, court her. He also finds that his applications to the Christminster colleges are ignored or rejected and, in bitterness, he gets drunk and, in a new 'abyss' of grief, decides to try to enter the church as a 'Licentiate' or clergyman of the lowest rank.

Sue goes to Melchester (Salisbury) to train as a teacher and Jude decides to go there to work as a stonemason, to prepare to attend the Theological College in that town and to be near her. Sue runs away from her training school and has a long talk with Jude; her behaviour to him constantly changes but it seems that she really has some feeling for him. In a fit of inexplicable emotion, however, she agrees to marry Phillotson, who has been courting her, and to work with him at a large school he has been given at Shaston (Shaftesbury). Sue asks Jude to 'give her away' at the ceremony, which he does. He visits his aunt again, who is dying, and goes back to Christminster where he meets Arabella, who has returned from Australia and is now working there as a barmaid.

Jude, however, does not take up with Arabella again and, indeed, visits Sue at her new married abode at Shaston. Partly under the influence of this visit, and partly on account of her growing distaste for Phillotson, she decides to leave her husband. When she does so she goes to live with Jude, though not as his wife. They both now divorce their former partners.

Sue and Jude are established in Aldbrickham (Reading) on the same basis as before when Arabella visits them briefly. Sue's jealousy is roused and she agrees both to sleep with Jude and to marry him and, although she does the former, she cannot bring herself to do the latter. Arabella, now married to a Mr Cartlett, asks Jude and Sue to take charge of her son, presumed to be Jude's son too, known as Little Father Time.

The public suspicion that they are not married drives Sue and Jude out of Aldrickham, and their financial position becomes more precarious. They settle in Kennetbridge where Jude falls ill. Arabella reappears, now a chapel-going widow. Phillotson, who has lost his good job at Shaston on account of his generous behaviour towards Sue, sets up again as a schoolmaster where he began, at Marygreen.

In the final part of the novel Jude and Sue have crept back to Christminster with Little Father Time, and two children of their own. Sue is pregnant again. It is summer and the end-of-year festivities are taking place (the Oxford 'Commem' period of boat races, balls and parties that concludes the academic year). The weather is damp, however, Jude is unwell and the family find it almost impossible to get lodgings. Little Father Time, always a blighted soul, hangs himself and the other two children, believing them to be contributory to the sorry state of the family. Sue then miscarries.

In her desperation Sue comes to believe that God is punishing her for her waywardness and she turns to religion suddenly and fervently. Arabella reappears once more. Sue decides that her real husband in the eyes of God is still Phillotson and she therefore remarries him and submits to him penitentially. Jude remarries Arabella in a mood of drunken despair but he further weakens his health by walking miles in the cold and the rain to visit Sue one last time. He dies in the summer when, once more, Christminster is celebrating.

Commentary

Jude was Hardy's last novel (although he revised and published *The Well-Beloved* in book form later) and it is his bleakest. It had a shrill and adversely critical reception of a kind that led Hardy to write in the Postscript to his Preface to the novel that 'the experience completely cur[ed] me of further interest in novel-writing'. Although nowadays the early reaction to the novel (which was called 'Jude the obscene', and thrown into the fire by a bishop) seems to us far-fetched and thoughtless, it has to be admitted that the bleakness of *Jude* can make it seem repellent. It offers an almost unrelieved picture of gloom and suggests a view of the universe in which malevolent fate thwarts all human aspirations. In contrast to *Far From the Madding Crowd*, and even *Tess, Jude* has no rural idyll to set against the pain of existence. There is no sheep-shearing supper, no Talbothays dairy – from the very first chapter both the social world and the natural world on which it is based are alien and hostile.

Thus Marygreen, which (being the smallest and most old-fashioned place in the novel, and the earliest-mentioned) might be expected to bear some similarity to Marlott (*Tess*) or Weatherbury (*Far From the Madding Crowd*), is described in the most dismal and even sarcastic terms. We see the village disturbed by the departure of the schoolmaster and abandoned for the day by the rector who is 'a man who disliked the sight of changes'. Jude, aged eleven, is in tears at his mentor's departure on this foggy morning. His aunt shouts at him to get on with bringing water from the village well and he does so, although the weight is almost too much for him and he has to walk to her cottage across a 'patch of clammy greensward'. The village itself is a mere hamlet, old and decayed:

> Old as it was, however, the well-shaft was probably the only relic of the local history that remained absolutely unchanged. Many of the thatched and dormered dwelling-houses had been pulled down of late years, and many trees felled on the green. Above all, the original church, hump-backed, wood-turreted, and quaintly hipped, had been taken down, and either cracked up into heaps of road-metal in the lane, or utilized as pig-sty walls, garden seats, guard-stones to fences, and rockeries in the flower-beds of the neighbourhood. In place of it a tall new building of modern Gothic design, unfamiliar to English eyes, had been erected on a new piece of ground by a certain obliterator of historic records who had run down from London and back in a day. The site whereon so long had stood the ancient temple to the Christian divinities was not even recorded on the green and level grass-plot that had immemorially been the churchyard, the obliterated graves being commemorated by eighteenpenny cast-iron crosses warranted to last five years.
>
> (*Jude the Obscure*, Part 1, Chapter 1)

This description is worth a careful study. It is a picture of decay and neglect and a picture of a new harsh world invading an old quaint one. The decay has been brought about by a migration, presumably to the great cities that grew up with the Industrial Revolution, and the village has been largely abandoned. The old church, which Hardy deliberately describes in pagan terms to stress that certain religious elements pre-date Christianity ('the ancient temple to the Christian divinities') symbolises the old way of life. The villagers have hung on to bits and pieces of the old life in the same way as they use pieces of the masonry of the church for casual purposes such as rockeries, but the spiritual centre of their world has been uprooted and replaced with something which does not belong to them (the architect has only visited the village for a few hours) and which is cheap, shoddy and temporary, as exemplified by the dreadful crosses that now stand to commemorate the village dead.

We have to be careful how we interpret such a passage. Hardy is not just harking back to the good old days when all was well between men. If that were the case episodes such as the pig-killing (Part 1, Chapter 10) would be out of place for such slaughtering forms an immemorial part of rural life; but as early as the second chapter of the novel, nature is already described in terms very different from those of *Under the Greenwood Tree*, say. Jude goes to the newly sown cornfield where his job is to scare away the birds.

> 'How ugly it is here!' he murmured. The fresh harrow-lines seemed to stretch like the channellings in a piece of new corduroy, lending a meanly utilitarian air to the expanse.
>
> (*Jude the Obscure*, Part I, Chapter 2)

The place itself seems blighted, and so it seems that we have now been offered two possibilities: first, that things have gone wrong because the modern world has spoiled the old world, and, second, that nature itself has not been kind to Marygreen. But Hardy does not let us rest with either of these, true though they both may be in their own way. He moves on to a more general indictment of nature and the universe.

Jude abandons his bird-scaring because of a sudden sympathy with the birds who, he feels, need to eat as much as he does and who 'seemed, like himself, to be living in a world which did not want them'. Jude is caught in this dereliction of his duty by the farmer and beaten; he goes home weeping and Hardy slips into his short list of possible reasons for these tears Jude's potential 'perception of the flaw in the terrestial scheme, by which what was good for God's birds was bad for God's gardener'. We begin to see in asides such as this the real bitterness towards the universe as a whole that motivates the novel. In some ways, certainly, modern consciousness is a burden on the characters, and the relationship between Jude and Sue, the principal centre of pain in the story, simply could not have developed as it did in an earlier period of history; getting married in the old days, according to Widow Edlin, was no more seriously regarded than 'a game o' dibs'. But on the other hand old-fashioned things can generate pain, too. Thus it is the primitive idea of a curse that is upon their family that forms a background of anxiety to the story of Jude and Sue, and Jude's aspirations are peculiarly dated: by the 1880s or 90s, when the novel is most probably set, there were plenty of other ways for an intelligent young man to get on instead of going to Oxford. Similarly it is the old-fashioned, almost medieval world of the Anglican High Church St Silas's that captures Sue's free soul in the end and the God she encounters there seems to be the fierce and vengeful deity of the Old Testament.

Really *Jude* is not set in Wessex at all. The nearest we get to the world of the earlier novels is the Great Wessex Agricultural Show, a mock version of the real Wessex just as Jude's and Sue's cakes are mock versions of Christminster. The 'ugly', different world of North Wessex, of Aldbrickham, of railways, is paralleled by the emancipating new world of John Stuart Mill (1806-73), the philosopher of liberty, and Registry Office weddings. Wessex has been left behind. As a result, Hardy's long loyalty to his native roots and to the gentle, humorous, quiet ways of the old Dorsetshire life, is at last broken and he can present his universe without indulging his taste for pastoral idyll. In *Jude* paradise is well and truly lost and Hardy seems able to make his point without having to consider more optimistic alternatives.

Points for study

---

1. *The design of the novel*
Hardy himself commented that there was potentially a much longer novel that could have been made out of the material of *Jude*. As it stands the novel is somewhat schematic (Hardy uses the word 'geometric') and is arranged almost like a square-dance with the characters changing partners at set points. Does this mar the work artistically? Is there any sense of rush or haste about any episodes or transitions? Do we feel that certain characters are brought in simply to make a point and then abandoned (the schoolmaster Gillingham, for instance)?

2. *Hardy's set pieces*
All novels contain a variety of scenes, but in *Jude* Hardy makes a point of building up certain elaborate pictures which are in the nature of icons or set pieces for our contemplation. Among these we can list: the pig-killing (Part 1, Chapter 10), the visit to the model of Jerusalem in Christminster (Part 2, Chapter 5), Sue and Jude painting the Ten Commandments (Part 5, Chapter 6), Jude addressing the 'populace' at Christminster when he finally returns there (Part 6, Chapter 1) and, of course, Jude quoting Job on his death-bed (Part 6, Chapter 11). Each of these, and there are plenty more, can be analysed as though it were a moral tableau, a picture to be deciphered so that we can discover Hardy's meaning. Thus: who is right in the pig-killing episode, Jude with his humane sympathy or Arabella with her 'poor folks must live'? What of the pig, the blood, the method of killing? When Arabella dirties Jude's boots with pig's grease is it accident, spite or a symbol for

the tarnishing of ideals by reality? Or again, when Jude visits the model of Jerusalem is he Christ (with his face deep in the Garden of Olives) or are we being asked simply to understand the strength of his imagination as he is lost in a reverie of what the real city must have been like? He can grasp neither Christminster nor Jerusalem to his satisfaction; if Jude is Christ then Hardy has chosen the right pseudonym for Oxford, but then we see that it rejects Jude as Jerusalem rejected Christ. At the end he is a Job crying to a God who has abandoned him. Do we believe in that God? If we do, Hardy seems to be saying, perhaps we need to reconsider our allegiance to such a cruel tyrant, and if we do not perhaps Hardy is offering us a metaphor for the workings of fate.

3. *Animals*
Jude is associated with birds and animals in several passages in the novel, as is Tess in her novel. Hardy's intention seems to be to associate Jude's sufferings with those of the animal kingdom in order to universalise his portrayal of the nature of things. As we have seen, Jude is involved with birds and with the pig in the first part of the novel. Later he is disturbed by rabbits caught in traps and Sue is highly distressed at having to sell her pigeons, 'A nice pie for somebody for next Sunday's dinner'. In this last episode (Part 5, Chapter 6) Hardy makes the universalising point explicit in Sue's exclamation: 'O why should Nature's law be mutual butchery!'

4. *Flesh and spirit*
There is a clear statement in the Preface that the novel is intended to be about 'a deadly war waged between flesh and spirit' and this is obvious enough in the way Jude is powerfully attracted both by the earthy Arabella and the 'epicene' Sue. This pattern (which applies to some extent to Phillotson, too) requires that Sue be a thing of spirit, of course, but this alone would be inadequate for Hardy's purposes: he is not writing a novel about a choice between, say, entering matrimony and entering a monastery. So Sue does have her own kind of sexuality but it is an ambiguous and puzzling one. She is a virgin when she marries, for, although she has lived with a man, the relationship was celibate. The man's death is hastened by Sue's 'holding out against him so long at such close quarters' but she claims that their relationship was almost that of 'two men'. There we have the ambiguity neatly caught. Sex is in the air and is powerful enough to kill, and Sue is unconventional enough to live with a man unmarried, but somehow she is unable to fulfil her femininity even though she knows that it would be better to be more normal. Jude points out that 'some women' would not have remained virgins under the circumstances: Sue replies

which extends from the most rational actions at one end, through emotions and passions to witchcraft at the other. He deliberately blurs the distinctions between them in the same way as he never makes it entirely clear whether he wants us to take Egdon Heath as being literally or only metaphorically malevolent.

That Susan is really trying serious witchcraft is apparent at her last effort in the novel when she recites the Lord's Prayer backwards and melts the image of Eustacia over the fire (Book 5, Chapter 7). It is left to us to decide what part this may play in Eustacia's death which follows so soon after.

The Mayor of Casterbridge (1886)

The plot

Michael Henchard, a hay-trusser in search of work, in a drunken state sells his wife and baby to a stranger at Weydon Priors fair. Some twenty years later this same wife returns to him together with their daughter, Elizabeth-Jane, now, of course, grown up. They bear the surname of the man who bought them, Newson, but they suppose him to have drowned during a voyage from Canada, where they had been living, and are now returning to seek out Henchard. 'Mrs Newson' has not told her daughter the full story but she has come to see that a purchase of Newson's sort hardly constitutes a proper marriage.

Henchard himself, having tried unsuccessfully to find his wife and daughter, has forsworn all alcoholic drink and has worked his way up to become the Mayor of Casterbridge (Dorchester, the county town of 'South Wessex'). He is pleased at the return of his wife and daughter and takes them in as soon as he is able to remarry his own wife. Meanwhile he has met and been very taken with a young Scotsman, Donald Farfrae, whom he has appointed his manager. All seems to be well except for the unfortunate fact that, in his wife's long absence, he has compromised a girl in Jersey, Lucetta, and has promised to marry her. He writes to her explaining his new position and sending her money; she accepts this but proposes to stop briefly at Casterbridge to collect from Henchard her letters to him. She is anxious to avoid any scandal that might further damage her prospects in life. Henchard has been extremely fond of his new manager, Farfrae, who has been paying his addresses to Elizabeth-Jane, but the two men fall out over a number of matters and Henchard forbids Elizabeth-Jane to continue to receive the Scotsman's attentions. Soon Mrs Henchard dies and Henchard is left alone with Elizabeth-Jane but when he explains to her, for the first time, that she is his daughter he immediately discovers, from a posthumous letter his wife has left for him, that the

Elizabeth-Jane he sold as a baby died and that this present Elizabeth-Jane is in fact the daughter of Newson. He conceals this from the girl but it sours his attitude towards her at just the moment when she has decided to accept him as her real father and behave like a true daughter.

Lucetta inherits some money, hears of Mrs Henchard's death, and comes to live in Casterbridge. She invites Elizabeth-Jane to come and live with her which the girl is glad to do now that Henchard is so cold towards her. Lucetta then meets Farfrae and becomes more interested in marrying him than in marrying Henchard as had been her original intention. They marry secretly. Henchard has been making mistakes in his business affairs, meanwhile, and he is becoming poorer while Farfrae grows richer. Once Henchard is bankrupt he tries to commit suicide but fails. Farfrae buys Henchard's house and moves into it with Lucetta. Henchard takes to drink again and is tended by Elizabeth-Jane. He drunkenly interrupts the reception of a 'Royal Personage' in Casterbridge and, feeling himself insulted by Farfrae, has a fight with him. Things are coming to a climax which is hastened by Lucetta's death: some of the rougher people in Casterbridge have discovered her earlier affair with Henchard and perform a 'skimmity-ride' outside her house, a custom which involves effigies of supposed adulterers being paraded outside their houses; the shock kills the pregnant Lucetta.

Newson now appears. He had given out false news of his own death to permit Mrs Henchard to return to her husband. Henchard tells him that his daughter, whom he is seeking, is dead. Henchard and Elizabeth-Jane are now living humbly together and running a small shop. Farfrae renews his attentions to Elizabeth-Jane and Newson appears again and meets her and tells her her true history. Henchard leaves Casterbridge and when he creeps back into the town for Elizabeth-Jane's marriage to Farfrae he is spoken to harshly by his stepdaughter and goes away again to die. His last words are conveyed to us by his despairing and pathetic last will and testament.

Commentary

The Mayor of Casterbridge is, more clearly than any of the other novels in this group, a novel of character. It is dominated by the personality, doings and even the physique of one man, Michael Henchard. He has the stature of a tragic hero: he is larger than life, a man of volcanic emotions and yet he is flawed, unpredictable, his own worst enemy. He loves and hates not wisely but too well and he conspires with his environment to bring his own fate upon himself. Hardy is evidently aware of this when he quotes, probably from George Eliot rather than directly from Novalis (Friederich von Hardenberg, 1772-1801), the aphorism 'Character is Fate' (Chapter 17). We feel about Tess, perhaps, that luck is against her and she only contributes a little towards her own undoing; Jude is more responsible for his fate but we feel that he, too, is an unlucky plaything of destiny; but Henchard, in his wrong-headed and emotional way, brings most of his misfortunes about single-handed. The wife-selling episode is the first example of this, but he continues to be almost equally impulsive even without the help of alcohol. His initial liking for Farfrae is almost absurdly strong, and in his affection for Elizabeth-Jane he blows hot and cold in a way that would have estranged anyone but a saint. A little more care in his dealing with people and in his commercial affairs would have assisted Henchard greatly.

Yet we like and pity this man. He is highly self-critical and seems almost too quick to agree that he deserves any punishment he gets: always stoical, after the revelation that Elizabeth-Jane is not his daughter he is assailed by the thought 'that the blasting disclosure was what he had deserved' (Chapter 19). He is, moreover, a good-hearted fellow of the most straightforward kind, as a magistrate for instance:

> . . . his rough and ready perceptions, his sledge-hammer directness, had often served him better than nice legal knowledge in despatching such simple business as fell to his hands
>
> (*The Mayor of Casterbridge*, Chapter 28)

And then his kindness is established by Abel Whittle, his mentally backward employee, who follows him faithfully at the end, remembering with gratitude Henchard's generosity to his old mother.

But being a good man, if you are also a headstrong and impulsive one, may not save you from the wrath of the gods. Perhaps there is a touch of divine vengeance in that Henchard is ultimately unable to escape the consequences of a bad deed committed years before; if so his story bears some resemblance to that of Oedipus and other tragic figures whose past catches up with them. Alternatively we may see Henchard as the victim of the wheel of fortune: he starts with nothing, rises to prosperity and power and descends to nothing again.

The novel almost entirely avoids Hardy's usual central topic – romantic and erotic love. It is perhaps this that generates the necessity for Henchard's personality to be a strongly emotional one. Strong motives are needed for tragedy, it seems, and in the absence of love Hardy finds it necessary to employ other powerful emotions such as friendship, and to increase their importance by establishing their possessor as an extreme character. This is one substitution that the author makes in his usual pattern; the other, of course, is the switch from such environments as Weatherbury and Egdon Heath to the urban scene of Casterbridge. Casterbridge is Dorchester, the centre of all things interesting to a boy born and brought up in a hamlet only three miles distant as Hardy was, and this is his opportunity to describe to us this town so familiar to him. In fact the life of the town hardly comes alive in the same way as the life of the villages and farms does in the other novels (up to but not including *Jude*). Hardy was perhaps most expert at painting small canvasses; thus the description of the Mixen Lane part of Casterbridge (Chapters 26 and 36) is masterly, as is the description of Henchard's house and its surroundings, but the sense of complete urban life is not altogether present in the novel. Perhaps this is not surprising, for Hardy is at pains to point out the very limited and old-fashioned nature of Casterbridge as a town.

> Casterbridge was the complement of the rural life around; not its urban opposite. Bees and butterflies in the cornfields at the top of the town, who desired to get to the meads at the bottom, took no circuitous course, but flew straight down High Street without any apparent consciousness that they were traversing strange latitudes.
> (*The Mayor of Casterbridge*, Chapter 9)

This novel, then, stands somewhat apart from Hardy's other major fiction in its stress on the character of its protagonist, the absence of a strong love interest and a more urban setting. The main themes of Hardy's work, however, are still present here: aspiration is thwarted by chance concatenations rather than by any human evil-doing, emotion is dangerous and calls up the wrath of the gods, events in towns obey the same laws as events in the country.

Points for study

1. *Elizabeth-Jane*
This young lady is no passionate Tess. Passion, and other dangers, are left to Lucetta among the women of the novel. Elizabeth-Jane is quiet, steady, sensible, unselfish, Christian, unambitious; the sort of person on whom the Furies find it hard to get a grip. It is no coincidence that it is Lucetta who dies and the second 'Mrs Farfrae' who survives.

A character such as this may seem untypical of Hardy after the vanities of Bathsheba Everdene and Fancy Day, not to mention such women as Tess Durbeyfield and Sue Bridehead. But she is not alone. Marty South, in *The Woodlanders*, is a humble, devoted and unambitious woman who survives, although she does suffer. Thomasin Yeobright in *The Return of the Native* is quiet and uncomplaining and not vain. Perhaps Elizabeth-Jane is a development of such a person as Liddy, Bathsheba's servant in *Far From the Madding Crowd*, too. It must be admitted, however, that she is not the most usual type of woman in Hardy's novels.

She is a very good, kind girl:

> If there was one good thing more than another which characterized this single-hearted girl it was a willingness to sacrifice her personal comfort and dignity to the common weal.
>
> (*The Mayor of Casterbridge*, Chapter 7)

She is aware that destiny can bring misfortune as well as fortune:

> 'I won't be too gay on any account', she would say to herself. 'It would be tempting Providence to hurl mother and me down, and afflict us again as He used to do.'
>
> (*The Mayor of Casterbridge*, Chapter 14)

She looks after Henchard generously in his misfortunes, and Hardy gives her the last two paragraphs of the novel. They bear some close scrutiny as it is clear that Hardy's own voice speaks in them.

2. The 'rustic chorus'

The chorus is not as developed here as in *Far From the Madding Crowd* or *The Return of the Native* but it still has a part to play. Hardy celebrates old Casterbridge, in the description of the Three Mariners inn, for instance (Chapter 6), and he sees the lesser townsfolk who frequent that establishment as part of an older life that goes about its business steadily beneath the more glamorous and dangerous surface of the world. Christopher Coney, Solomon Longways and the others are cheerful, amusing, and keep to their own humble places as watchers of the action rather than participants. When Hardy needs an element of the populace to bring off his *coup de théâtre*, the 'skimmity-ride', he calls on the less benign inhabitants of Mixen Lane and limits the involvement of the 'worthies' of the Three Mariners to the sending of an anonymous note that is intended to save Lucetta from shame but may have helped to hasten her death. When Lucetta is buried Christopher Coney digs up the four pennies that have been placed on her eyelids and spends them in the inn asking the philosophical question 'Why should death rob life o' fourpence?'

3. Shakespeare

In this as in other novels Hardy reminds us from time to time that he has Shakespearean situations and elements at the back of his mind. The most obvious example here comes at the end of the novel where Henchard makes something of a King Lear figure: the despairing old man driven out by his daughter onto a heath, accompanied only by his faithful but foolish follower, reminds us irresistibly of Shakespeare's tragic hero. Another example, from the other end of Shakespeare's range as it were, is provided by the Casterbridge constables, Stubbard and Blowbody (Chapter 39), who are highly reminiscent of the comic constables Dogberry and Verges in *Much Ado About Nothing*. In general it is useful to look for points of comparison between Shakespeare and Hardy, who knew his work well.

4. *Old Testament*

Like Jude, though perhaps a little less frequently, Henchard is associated with such Old Testament characters as Job (Chapter 40 for instance), Cain (Chapter 43) and Samson (44). These victims of God's anger, whose names appear more frequently in the later parts of the novel, are clearly Old Testament symbols of suffering men not dissimilar from that secular symbol of the same type, King Lear. The final symbol, besides Lear, is probably the goldfinch (Chapter 45) which is starved to death by a combination of accidents for which it is not responsible. Its death makes it seem that it is a symbol of Henchard's soul, coming as it does so soon before his own death and having been, as it were, his final attempt to make peace with the world.

The Woodlanders (1887)

The plot

Mr Melbury, a timber merchant in the South Wessex village of Little Hintock, has promised his daughter Grace in marriage to Giles Winterborne. Grace returns home after an expensive education, and some travel, a somewhat changed young woman; and Melbury regrets his promise, but determines to stick to it. A poor girl from the village, Marty South, also regrets it as she is in love with Giles herself.

A new doctor, Edred Fitzpiers, has recently settled in the village. He becomes interested in Grace but later he will also be attracted to Mrs Charmond, an old flame of his who lives at Hintock House, and is the local landowner and a widow. A struggle now ensues in various quarters. Melbury has to force himself to keep the vow he made to Giles's father that Giles should have Grace. Fitzpiers has to decide between the upper-class life of Mrs Charmond, and his own family, on the one hand, and his attraction to Grace on the other. Marty has to contain her feelings. Grace, who has been taken up by Mrs Charmond, also has to decide to which class she wishes to belong.

Marty South's father dies, and as a result Giles Winterborne is turned out of his house, which was only held on 'life-hold' until the old man's death. Melbury and Grace, after some changes in her moods, decide that she should not marry Winterborne. He plays a smaller part in the novel for the next dozen chapters or so, and Fitzpiers's courtship of Grace is described; Fitzpiers, besides courting Grace, is carrying on an affair with Suke Damson, a village girl, and it is only by a quick lie that he is able to prevent Grace from breaking with him when she is on the verge of discovering this affair. They are married and after their honeymoon they have to settle into Hintock life, somewhat to Fitzpiers's disgust. He plans to move to Budmouth but his offer to buy a practice there is suddenly withdrawn when Mrs Charmond returns to the village and he discovers her to be his old love. They start an affair that naturally estranges Fitzpiers from Grace. Grace quickly sees that there is something between her husband and Mrs Charmond and discovers that Suke Damson has also been involved with him. She starts to regret her fine education and to pity Giles who is now working as an itinerant cider-maker. Mr Melbury appeals to Mrs Charmond, asking her to leave Fitzpiers alone, as does Grace, and she wishes sincerely to do so but is too much in love with him. A series of accidents, including a fall from a horse and a bizarre argument with Melbury, leaves Fitzpiers lying injured at Hintock House with Mrs Charmond. Thrown together thus the two of them go away to Europe together and simply abandon the scene of battle.

Melbury, feeling guilty at his part in bringing about this disaster, and hearing of a new divorce law (the Matrimonial Causes Act of 1857 is probably what Hardy had in mind), goes to London from where he writes to Grace that she is to forget Fitzpiers and to encourage Winterborne again, which she is now quite willing to do. Their one passionate kiss is exchanged between Grace and Giles before Melbury returns from London with the news that there can be no divorce after all.

Fitzpiers returns from the Continent after a rupture with Mrs Charmond, who has been shot by another jealous lover. Grace, feeling she cannot meet him, takes refuge in Giles Winterborne's hut in the woods, Giles out of propriety prefering to live exposed to the bad weather and sleep under a mere shelter. As a result Giles, whose health has not been good, dies of a fever and Grace is prostrated. She and Marty meet regularly at his grave but after a time she returns to Fitzpiers, who has set up in a Midlands town, and Marty is left to tend the grave alone.

Commentary

As in his other novels, we find Hardy in *The Woodlanders* using the technique of bringing an outsider into the humble ways of Wessex life. Outside forces bring tragedy in their wake, and there is a sense at the end that people would have perhaps done better to have remained contented with things as they were. In this connection it is worth quoting the stanza from Gray's (1716-71) 'Elegy in a Country Churchyard' that provided Hardy with the title for another novel:

Far from the madding crowd's ignoble strife
  Their sober wishes never learnt to stray;
Along the cool sequestered vale of life
  They kept the noiseless tenor of their way.

Hardy's country folk might have avoided tragedy if they had kept their wishes 'sober' and, remaining in the remote vales of Wessex, had plodded noiselessly through life. In *Jude*, obviously enough, it is Jude's ambition that drives him into difficulties; the village lad, who dreams of becoming a scholar and a bishop, exposes himself, at the very least, to the possibility of disappointment. Outside the quiet village lies danger. Similarly in *Tess* things go wrong because John Durbeyfield is told that he might really be a gentleman and because Tess goes from Marlott to Trantridge to 'claim kin' and falls in with Alec d'Urberville. By the same token, in *The Woodlanders*, it is the presence in Little Hintock of Fitzpiers and Mrs Charmond, and the return there of Grace Melbury, that brings about the suffering in which so many of the characters share.

Fitzpiers is a man with some local connexions but he is utterly alien to the life of the Hintock woods. Hardy emphasises this almost to the point of exaggeration and has Fitzpiers quoting Shelley and the seventeenth-century philosopher Spinoza (the latter in Latin) in his first conversation with Winterborne (Chapter 16) while at the same time stressing his medical and scientific interests, his wide reading and his travel. Mrs Charmond has been long absent from the village which she largely owns, and, as she dislikes it, she escapes abroad as often as possible; her involvement, symbolically, is to demolish the villagers' houses and to purchase Marty's hair for her own adornment; her distance from the woodlanders in terms of social class is everywhere apparent, not least in her interview with Mr Melbury when the latter wishes to persuade her to put an end to her affair with Fitzpiers. Grace Melbury, as is stressed again and again, has been educated in new ways that bear no resemblance to the ways of Hintock: she feels at home with Mrs Charmond and is at variance with the friends of her girlhood in terms of her language, her manners, her social life and her expectations.

Hardy, then, is only telling half the truth when he describes the village in these terms:

It was one of those sequestered spots outside the gates of the world where may usually be found more meditation than action, and more listlessness than meditation; where reasoning proceeds on narrow premises, and results in inferences wildly imaginative; yet where, from time to time, dramas of a grandeur and unity truly Sophoclean are enacted in the real, by virtue of the concentrated passions and closely-knit interdependence of the lives therein.

(*The Woodlanders*, Chapter 1)

This describes the novel up to a point, but it omits the fact that the 'Sophoclean' tragedy is brought about far more by the intrusion of outside forces than by the close ties that exist within the community of the village. Perhaps the best example of this may be found in the question of Grace's possible divorce: Melbury goes to London, where all is confusion for him, and the remote gods of the law decree, randomly it seems, what shall be Grace's fate; back in Hintock this decree from without will result in Giles' death and a future for Grace and Fitzpiers just the opposite of what we have briefly expected.

Perhaps *The Woodlanders* can best be seen, then, as a study of two opposing ways of life, of the cosmopolitan, urban, educated, 'outside' world and of the isolated Wessex villagers; this is the 'old world' being invaded by the new, of course, and it represents both what happened in Dorset during Hardy's lifetime and the two aspects of Hardy himself. It is easy to forget how well educated and urbane Hardy was: the view that has him well-nigh a peasant is utterly at odds with his knowledge of Greek and his indefatigable attendance at London dinner-parties.

It must not be thought, however, that Hardy either takes sides in this debate or that he believes that nature would do so. He does not condemn the town and praise the country, he does not show more sympathy or understanding for one set of characters than for the other. The clash of the 'outside' world with the life of the Hintock dwellers is not the invasion of a rural paradise by uncaring and destructive sophisticates. To some extent Mrs Charmond, in particular, may seem uncaring and destructive, but against that we must set Hardy's presentation of the woods and life within them. The opening of Chapter 4, with its images of death and blood, makes this explicit enough, as does the description of Grace and her father passing through the woods in Chapter 7. In this latter passage Hardy makes his impartiality absolutely clear:

Here, as everywhere, the Unfulfilled Intention, which makes life what it is, was as obvious as it could be among the depraved crowds of a city slum. The leaf was deformed, the curve was crippled, the taper was interrupted; the lichen ate the vigour of the stalk, and the ivy slowly strangled to death the promising sapling.

(*The Woodlanders*, Chapter 7)

Hardy carefully chooses words, such as 'deformed' and 'crippled', which stress the links between the city slum and the woodlands: the slum child may be 'crippled' and he, too, may be a 'promising sapling' that will not grow to his full potential.

Grace Melbury is the pivot of all this, just as Tess Durbeyfield is in her novel. Grace, even more than Tess, is a cut above her family and so resides in an uncomfortable limbo between the social classes. Under the circumstances, and considering the fates of Tess and Eustacia Vye for example, she is lucky to escape with her life.

Points for study

---

1. *Giles Winterborne*
He can be compared with Gabriel Oak in his closeness to nature, but Hardy's vision has darkened in the years since *Far From the Madding Crowd* and Giles does not seem to possess the power for survival that closeness to nature gives Gabriel Oak. He is 'born in winter', an unlucky man without the oak's deep-rooted hold on life, so that, although he is stoical and a good tree-planter, he becomes discouraged and ill sooner than his earlier prototype. And yet the description of him making cider (opening paragraphs of Chapter 25) seems to blend him inextricably with the near-natural process in which he is engaged; he is 'autumn's very brother' (Chapter 28) and here he represents 'naturalised' man at his most extreme, being paralleled in Hardy's work only by Clym Yeobright in *The Return of the Native*, working on the heath, utterly involved in its insect and plant life.

2. *Marty South*
Marty is perhaps another Fanny Robin, the secondary heroine of *Far From the Madding Crowd*, but if so then she and Fanny reverse the positions of Gabriel Oak and Giles Winterborne, for Fanny dies a miserable death while Marty survives stoically. Marty is a great worker, a simple but determined girl who stands in contrast to Mrs Charmond's luxurious idleness. The pattern, of course, in which she is caught up, is part of 'the great web of human doings then weaving in both hemispheres from the White Sea to Cape Horn' (*The Woodlanders*, Chapter 3). The extent of this web begins to become apparent to us as we realise that she loves Giles, who loves Grace, who loves Fitzpiers, who loves Mrs Charmond . . . . Marty can also be compared with Elizabeth-Jane in *The Mayor of Casterbridge*; each of these stoical girls, at any rate, survives and concludes her novel.

3. *Humanity*
Hardy is strongly disinclined to blame anyone for the tragedies that befall his characters. Certain desires and courses of action may be the immediate causes of suffering but there is always the sense of some powerful force or fate *behind* human action, propelling it forward. 'Poor, hard-run humanity' is thus everywhere to be pitied rather than

censured, and we find symbol of this in *The Woodlanders*, Chapter 33. Here Mrs Charmond and Grace Melbury have a heated argument about the affair between Mrs Charmond and Fitzpiers, now Grace's husband; but it is a cold March night and they get lost in the woods so that, although they have parted in anger, they are glad enough, when they meet again, to rest together, even to cling to one another for warmth. Grace who had been 'sick with distaste' for the other woman earlier in the chapter, now presses herself against Mrs Charmond's furs and holds her. When Mrs Charmond reveals that she and Fitzpiers have made love, Grace rises and wishes to leave her companion,

> But Felice Charmond's sobs came to her ear: deep darkness circled her about, the cold lips of the wind kissed her where Mrs. Charmond's warm fur had been, and she did not know which way to go.

(The Woodlanders, Chapter 33)

Grace turns back to her companion and they leave the wood together. In the passage quoted Hardy makes it clear the reasons for this turn of events come in a certain order: first one human being hears the distress signal of another (the sobbing), then the darkness is mentioned and the very natural human desire to have another person by in such circumstances. Then, like so may people so much of the time, Grace is lost, she does not know which way to go in a hostile world and turns to Mrs Charmond, her enemy, for companionship. Any human, it seems, is one's friend in the face of the implacable universe. Against such a background blame becomes an unworthy consideration. Mrs Charmond insists to Grace that she *'cannot'* give Fitzpiers up: her love is another of those external forces against which we struggle so vainly, it is not her fault.

4. *The rustic chorus*

The Woodlanders deals with some events in the lives of fairly humble folk (Marty South, Giles himself), and perhaps for this reason does not have a very highly developed rustic chorus. To such as Mrs Charmond *all* the Hintock villagers must seem equally rustic, with Fitzpiers, and perhaps Grace, standing out from the throng. Melbury, in fact, inhabits what was the old manor house of the village (before Mrs Charmond's estate expanded) and belongs to that class to which Hardy fancied he belonged himself: prosperous, not a mere peasant, but very local and not at all 'gentry', yet it is obvious that Mrs Charmond fails to make much of this distinction. A rustic chorus of the traditional Hardy kind, however, is present in the shape of Robert Creedle, Giles Winterborne's humorous and sometimes 'tragic' servant who reminds us of Joseph Poorgrass in *Far From the Madding Crowd* or the clientele of the Three Mariners in *The Mayor of Casterbridge*. His role in the novel, that of deflating moments of tragedy, serves only to heighten our sadness in the end. He comes into his own, particularly, in Chapters 9 and 10.

Under the Greenwood Tree (1872)

The plot

The novel opens on Christmas Eve. The 'Mellstock Quire', that is, the choir, singers and instrumentalists of the South Wessex village of Mellstock, go carol-singing and are thanked for their pains by the pretty new schoolmistress, Fancy Day. They are then cursed by a farmer, Mr Shiner, and thanked by the handsome new parson, Maybold. Dick Dewy, son of the 'tranter' or carrier, Reuben Dewy, is much struck by the sight of Fancy Day at her window and he determines to court her. On Christmas Day Dick sits next to Fancy at a party in his father's house and later dances with her.

In the spring the parson, Maybold, decides that the instrumental part of the choir should be disbanded and replaced by an organ. After some negotiations, and much distress on the part of the players, it is agreed that the change will take place at Michaelmas (in September) and that Fancy Day will play the organ.

The scene now shifts to Fancy's father's house in Yalbury Wood. Geoffrey Day works as a keeper and general estate agent and lives in a pretty cottage. Keeper Day has an eccentric wife but in spite of her disagreeable ways Dick, who has come to the cottage to collect Fancy and the furniture for her school-house at Mellstock, is well pleased to see Fancy at home and to drive her back to the village. He begins, however, to have fears about her interest in Farmer Shiner and, although his courtship prospers well enough in the following months, he learns that Keeper Day has started to encourage Shiner as a prospective son-in-law.

Dick becomes a little frustrated by Fancy's vanity and inconstancy, but they do seem to love one another, so Dick, according to plan, goes to call on Keeper Day, who manages to convince him that he is not rich enough for his daughter. Fancy, depressed by this paternal opposition, is advised to pretend to be ill and thus frighten her father into agreement, a piece of advice which succeeds admirably. But then, suddenly, Parson Maybold proposes marriage to his young organist and she, overwhelmed by this chance of a substantial rise in social status, accepts him. When, however, the parson discovers by accident that she is already betrothed to Dick he sends her a note cancelling their engagement with which she concurs. In the last scene of the novel

Dick and Fancy are married and she has not told him of her brief engagement to Maybold.

Commentary

Hardy is completely in his element in this, his shortest and happiest novel. He is, in fact, literally 'at home' in that Mellstock is modelled on the villages, such as Stinsford and the Bockhamptons, in which he grew up; Reuben Dewy's house is a replica of Hardy's parents' home (still standing) and the 'quire' represents some of Hardy's earliest memories and recollections of the tales of his father and grandfather.

He had tried a social and satirical novel (*The Poor Man and the Lady*, 1868, later destroyed) and had followed advice to write something 'sensational' in publishing his first printed novel (*Desperate Remedies*, 1871) but he had also been advised that the country scenes in *The Poor Man and the Lady* were the best part of that novel. *Under the Greenwood Tree*, then, avoids satire and, indeed, urban and upper-class social life altogether, and, remembering the failure of *Desperate Remedies*, which had not done well, avoids the sensationalism and violence of that novel. Hardy had not yet found his later technique which enabled him to picture the universe as he really saw it, and so excluding both satire and sensationalism meant to him painting a largely cheerful picture. The second subtitle of the novel, 'A Rural Painting of the Dutch School', implies a self-confident and loving depiction of the humble and humorous detail of village and country life. In later novels Hardy was able to amalgamate the satire, and sensationalism and the pastoralism and, adding a good deal more besides, to write his most powerful novels. *Under the Greenwood Tree*, therefore, shows him still in the development stage, experimenting on a deliberately restricted canvas.

The novel seems to consist, when one looks back at it from the perspective of later works, almost entirely of a 'rustic chorus'. The 'quire' is basically made up of attractively humorous rustics who, although here they may sometimes seem to be caricatures, are the true originals of the 'chorus' characters that appear, particularly, in *Far From the Madding Crowd* and *The Return of the Native*. Dick Dewy, Parson Maybold, Farmer Shiner and Keeper Day (when Dick himself is older he will presumably come to be called 'Tranter Dewy') are all of a higher social status than the basic quire members, as their common appellations imply, but, except perhaps for the parson, who plays only a small part in the story and seems in some ways to belong to a different species, these people have almost everything in common with the villagers. Shiner, for example, joins in the Christmas party at the Dewys' easily enough and Keeper Day speaks with the Wessex accent.

Fancy, of course, is a somewhat more educated young lady but whereas her literary successor in the Hardy canon – Grace Melbury in *The Woodlanders* – is put in a position where tragedy must follow from her ambiguous social status, Fancy seems all along to accept that Dick Dewy and the village life he represents are a desirable prospect.

Nonetheless, in spite of the cohesion evident in the novel, in spite of the benevolent tradition of mutual assistance that Hardy ascribes to the people of Mellstock, we can feel the seeds of his later tragedies sprouting here. Dick Dewy in love is a picture of suffering: jealousy and frustration are not far below the surface. Fancy's vanity, her desire for improved social position, nearly lead her into a marriage that seems to offer her only dubious satisfactions. Above all, the law of nature, that men will compete for an attractive woman who enters their environment, to the inevitable disappointment of all the men save one, is steadily exemplified. The pattern of the later novels is there.

There is some doubt, in the first half of the novel at least, as to whether Hardy takes the fate of the 'quire' or the fate of Fancy Day in love as his principal theme and, although this doubt is finally resolved in favour of love, it too indicates that the pattern of the later novels is present here. If we compare this novel with *Jude the Obscure*, for instance, we see that there, too, there is a question as to whether Hardy is more concerned with the social matters of Jude's aspiration, education and marriage or with the emotional question of his relationship with Sue. In *Under the Greenwood Tree* the fate of the 'quire' is surely an embryo social question and what is most typically Hardyesque is the way in which this question and the question of love are woven together. The 'great web' in this short novel may not be as elaborately woven by Hardy as it was to be later but it is still in evidence: the 'quire's' carol-singing brings Dick his first sight of Fancy and its breaking-up leads to her dangerous relationship with Maybold. These things might have come about under any circumstances, 'quire' or no 'quire', but the deliberate linkages show Hardy experimenting with what was to become his most characteristic technique: the weaving together of the strands of destiny that enmesh the whole of life. It is perhaps for this reason that Hardy included *Under the Greenwood Tree* among his 'Novels of Character and Environment' rather than, say, among the 'Romances and Fantasies' where it might seem more naturally to belong.

Points for study

---

1. *Description*
There are many excellent descriptive passages in *Under the Greenwood Tree* that repay study. For example: the opening of the novel (Part 1,

Chapter 1) with its unusual description of the trees on a windy night and its characteristic technique of presenting first nature, then an anonymous person, then others, slowly to the reader (Hardy's novels characteristically do *not* open with the *curriculum vitae* of the hero); the description of the tranter's house (Part 1, Chapter 2) which can be compared with one of Hardy's earliest surviving poems, 'Domicilium'; the description of the dancing (Part 1, Chapter 7), a *tour de force* on a notoriously difficult topic; the description of Keeper Day's house (Part 2, Chapter 6) which again shows Hardy's mastery of detail; the description of the honey-taking (Part 4, Chapter 2).

2. *Dialogue*

It may come as something of a surprise to us to realise that the greater part of this novel consists of dialogue. Hardy is quite brilliant at all types of dialogue and he particularly excels at the talk of his rustics. Scenes such as the interview between the 'quire' and Parson Maybold (Part 2, Chapter 4) seem almost as if they could have been written for the stage. The penultimate chapter (Part 5, Chapter 1) is a complex series of conversations carried on between people in different rooms and across fields and it works very well as an account of the preparations of the villagers and of Fancy and Dick for their wedding.

3. *Details*

In this early novel Hardy as it were tries out some of the motifs that are going to become of more importance and of greater use to him later. For instance we find him allowing certain characters the privilege of *seeing unseen*, of *spying*, a motif which will reappear in *Far From the Madding Crowd* and elsewhere (see *Under the Greenwood Tree* Part 1, Chapter 6, 'The gallery of Mellstock Church . . .' and Part 4, Chapter 2, passim). Similarly he employs the device of the *barrier between lovers*, the conversation through the window, for instance (see Part 1, Chapter 5 and Part 4, Chapter 6), which will feature also in *The Woodlanders* and *Jude the Obscure*. Then there is the association of *bright shiny colours* with dubious character, which we will find again in Alec d'Urberville and Sergeant Troy, found here in the name and appearance of Farmer Shiner (see Part 1, Chapter 7 and Part 3, Chapters 1 and 2). Such details and motifs, when repeated, provide useful clues to the understanding of Hardy's fiction.

Chapter 5

'Romances and Fantasies'

A Pair of Blue Eyes (1873)

The plot

Stephen Smith, a young architect's assistant from London, visits Endelstow, in a remote part of Off-Wessex (Cornwall) to advise the Rector there, Mr Swancourt, about the restoration of his church. Stephen is at once attracted to Elfride, Mr Swancourt's daughter, and she to him. He makes a good impression on the rector, too, and is invited to return for another visit. When he returns, his love for Elfride prospers and they become virtually engaged, but he is then forced to reveal that he is the son of John Smith, a mason working for the nearby landowner and relative of the Swancourts, Lord Luxellian. This appals the snobbish rector who more or less turns him out of the house. Elfride, who has been forbidden to think of marrying him, decides to go to London and there marry him secretly. They meet in Plymouth and take the train to London but once there Elfride changes her mind, or loses her courage, and insists on returning immediately to Plymouth and to Endelstow. Her absence has not been noticed by her father who has, coincidentally, gone away from home himself at the same time, to be married secretly.

We are now introduced to Henry Knight, a successful London man of letters and barrister, who has acted as mentor and tutor to Stephen and whom the latter worships. It turns out that he is a distant relative of the new Mrs Swancourt who invites him to Endelstow where he, of course, meets Elfride and proves to be the reviewer who has savaged her first attempt at fiction – an Arthurian romance she has published under a pseudonym. After some differences between them Knight and Elfride begin to fall in love. Stephen, who is still entirely devoted to Elfride, has gone to Bombay to improve his prospects. He sends money home to Elfride, but by the time he comes himself she is partially committed to Knight, whose life she has been instrumental in saving. Stephen has to watch her and Knight together, and it is Knight himself who tells Stephen that he and Elfride are engaged to be married. Stephen returns to India but Elfride is still to some degree watched over by the witch-like figure of Mrs Jethway, the mother of an Endelstow boy who has died of consumption, but who, she thinks, has died of unrequited love for Elfride before the arrival of Stephen.

On a boat trip from London to Plymouth Elfride learns that Henry Knight, her fiancé, has never kissed a woman before he kissed her, except his mother, and that he insists on an almost equal purity in his bride-to-be. Mrs Jethway, who has discovered the facts of Elfride's aborted elopement with Stephen, threatens to betray them to Knight which, considering the consternation he manifests when told only of a kiss, seems very dangerous to Elfride's prospects with him. The old woman dies, apparently by her own hand, but leaves behind her a letter which tells Knight all. Knight breaks off the engagement and leaves Endelstow. Elfride, re-enacting an old pattern, follows him to London but this time she is followed and brought back by her father.

Stephen prospers in India and returns. Knight travels on the continent and remains embittered. He and Stephen meet in London and at last Knight discovers that Elfride's earlier elopement had been with his young friend. The love of both men for Elfride is rekindled by their conversation and they travel by train down to 'Off-Wessex', each with the intention of proposing to her again. They travel in the same train as Elfride's corpse, however, for she, despairing of Knight and perhaps of Stephen, too, has fallen ill, married Lord Luxellian, gone abroad with him and died during a miscarriage in London.

Commentary

A Pair of Blue Eyes is in some respects a dramatisation of Hardy's own courtship of his first wife, Emma Gifford. As such it is perhaps surprising that in it he adopts a tone of mild satire towards and detachment from the action of the novel. The result is that we are never caught up in the emotional dilemmas of the characters in the way that we are in Tess of the d'Urbervilles, for instance. A Pair of Blue Eyes is not unsuccessful as a novel but it lacks the seriousness of Hardy's major work. Elfride, for instance, is not carefully built up into a marked, fated, tragic victim as Tess is (or even as Eustacia Vye is to some degree). Her death seems a little casual in contrast with the deaths of these other heroines, and the sufferings of her lovers are to some extent diminished by the lightness of her personality (she does not quite convince us of her ability to arouse grand passions in the way Tess and Sue Bridehead do) as well as by some aspects of her lovers' characters. Thus Stephen Smith is young, naïve, stiff and too much of a puppy for us to sympathise with him, while Henry Knight is rather absurd in his priggishness.

It is worth stressing these limitations in the emotional range of the novel. The student of Hardy has to accept the work for what it is and thus be able to appreciate it for its own merits. First, it demonstrates a number of themes and interests of Hardy's very clearly, and, second, it works well as a satire, even as a comedy, in spite of its tragic *dénouement*.

The themes of the novel are inconstancy and constancy in love, class and concealment, and the nature of woman. The first of these centres round Elfride. She is inconstant and, although the novel focuses on the fickleness of her love for Stephen when she agrees to marry Knight, this is not the only example we are offered: there is a suggestion that she has been unfaithful to Felix Jethway; she is inconstant in her attachment to Stephen even while she still loves him, agreeing to elope with him at one moment and then asking to be taken home at another; she may even seem unfaithful to Knight when she marries Lord Luxellian. The trouble is that she loves being loved and does not seem able to hold to her purpose in loving when a new man appears and offers her the drug she craves. This psychological defect is at the bottom of the accusation of 'vanity' that Hardy levels both at Elfride and at Bathsheba Everdene.

Constancy, of course, is manifested in Stephen whom we find, in his hotel in Pimlico, reading through Elfride's old letters, which he has kept about him, although, as far as he knows, she has been married to Knight for a couple of years.

Class is a continually recurring topic in Hardy, and in this novel we have the familiar situation of the 'poor man' (here an architect, as in *A Laodicean*) aspiring to the hand of the 'lady'. It appears, ironically, that Stephen Smith's father may be better off financially than Mr Swancourt, that, at least, is what Elfride claims when she is forbidden to marry him, but Mr Swancourt finds the prospect of his daughter marrying the son of a stonemason quite horrifying. And it is from this class-consciousness that the need for concealment arises: Stephen conceals his origins from the Swancourts for as long as he can, and when he can no longer do so he feels driven to attempt a secret marriage. Mr Swancourt, too, conceals his proposed marriage to Mrs Troyton from his daughter until it has safely taken place.

The third theme, the nature of woman, is perhaps the commonest single theme in Victorian fiction and was certainly close to Hardy's heart. In this novel, in particular, he seems determined to present the widest possible range of possible female roles in the person of Elfride. She is a goddess and a little girl, a queen and a suppliant, extraordinarily changeable. For Stephen she is '*La Belle Dame sans merci*' (Chapter 7) but we have seen her, just before his arrival, an anxious girl-housekeeper under her father's thumb; for Knight she is isolated rustic innocence, a virgin mind and body, utterly his inferior and to be taught everything by him, and yet she is an accomplished horsewoman and musician (probably better than Knight on both these counts), a novelist and a reasonable chess player, capable of the resourceful and energetic action that saves his life when he, foolishly, nearly falls over a steep cliff; she is subject to a man when she loves him but almost delights in subjugating any man while she is deciding whether to love him or not; she has the courage to escape twice to London but once there either loses her nerve or allows herself to be fetched home by her father. Hardy uses a wide range of vocabulary in describing Elfride and her actions, typified in his comment at the moment when her affection switches from Stephen to Knight: 'It was infinitely more to be even the slave of the greater than the queen of the less' (Chapter 22).

Points for study

---

1. *The scenery*

'Off-Wessex', being Cornwall, afforded Hardy more dramatic scenery than was to be found in 'South Wessex' (Dorset). He was to make much out of some of the stretches of heathland that existed near his birthplace, expanding them into the ominous landscape of Egdon Heath, but in Cornwall (where he had first gone, after all, only a couple of years before starting on *A Pair of Blue Eyes*) he found immense cliffs and Atlantic breakers ready to hand. To some extent he simply ignored them and the general tone of his descriptions of life in Endelstow village is little different from that of his usual depiction of Dorset villages – we meet the same rustics who talk in the same way, for instance – but he does put the North Cornish coast to use in certain ways. First, he is able, on account of the absence of railways in the area at that date, to emphasise the isolation of the place and this helps him to set up the necessary tensions between town and country and between sophistication and innocence. Second, he seizes on the cliffs for the most dramatic episode in the novel (Chapters 21 and 22). Third, he adds to Elfride's complexity and personifies her impulsiveness by having her ride somewhat recklessly about this wild and remote countryside. However, Hardy makes less use of landscape and scenery in this novel than he does in later and greater works such as *The Return of the Native*, *Tess of the d'Urbervilles* and *The Woodlanders*. This reluctance to weave action and landscape together in what was to become the hallmark of his mature style results in *A Pair of Blue Eyes* seeming less serious and powerful than those other novels.

2. *The cliff episode*

Chapters 21 and 22 are a *tour de force* of suspense writing (almost literally: we hold our breath while Knight hangs on to his life by a tuft of grass) but they also contain the most serious philosophising passage that Hardy permits himself in this 'romance'. The first ten paragraphs of Chapter 22 form a fascinating meditation made all the more serious by the predicament of Knight through whose mind it passes. Even students of Hardy who are unable to enjoy reading this novel as a whole should make a careful analysis of this remarkable piece of writing. In particular it is worth sorting out the different strands of his style which shifts, even in these desperate straits, from such phrases as 'the inveterate antagonism of these black precipices to all struggles for life', which reminds us of the most sombre parts of the description of Egdon Heath in the opening chapter of *The Return of the Native*, to such details as the fossilised trilobite that seems to be looking at Knight and which Hardy calls 'this underling'. The passage is not entirely without humour. It also contains, however, a *résumé* of the evolutionary process and a series of thoughts on the nature of time that help us to see the depth of Hardy's perspective on life.

The twelfth paragraph of Chapter 22 offers as good a summary of Hardy on the subject of 'Nature' as we will find anywhere in his novels, distanced by being recorded as the opinion of 'West-country folk'. The paragraph begins 'To those musing . . . '.

3. *Hardy's fetishism*

Hardy catches the obsessive nature of love by stressing the importance of certain physical objects. In *Under the Greenwood Tree* there is the last on which the cobbler, Penny, will make a shoe for Fancy Day's foot, fascinating to Dick Dewy. In *A Pair of Blue Eyes* there are the two pairs of earrings, given to Elfride by Stephen and Knight respectively, which act as talismans in the loves of these three people. Knight, in particular, spends an inordinate amount of time and money on his present and the scene in which he asks if he may put the earrings on Elfride himself almost develops into a ritual of domination and submission (Chapter 28). The involuntary kiss that follows the earring episode turns out to be Knight's first kiss of a sexual kind and we are made to feel that the earrings have played an immense part in sealing the love of these two people. Shoe-lasts and earrings are not the only fetishistic objects in Hardy; their significance is worth pondering.

4. *Hardy's feminism*

Hardy judges no one and blames no one, but he is exceptionally clear-minded in his view of the relations of men and women and in *A Pair of Blue Eyes*, as later in *Tess of the d'Urbervilles*, he shows how, among the many 'circumstances' that beset women, the selfish and absurd behaviour of men plays a crucial part. Stephen we may forgive, and Mr Swancourt seems to expect obedience from his daughter in a patchy and fairly normal way for a nineteenth-century parson, but Knight dominates and even torments Elfride on the grounds of his superior sex, age and education in a way that readers may well find offensive.

The Trumpet-Major (1880)

The plot

Anne Garland lives with her widowed mother at Overcombe in South Wessex, not far from the south coast of England. They live in part of an old mill worked by Miller Loveday who has two sons, John, a Trumpet-Major (non-commissioned officer) in the army, and Bob, a sailor.

It is the time of the Napoleonic wars and everyone is nervous about the supposedly imminent invasion of England by the French (which sets the novel in about 1804). Several army regiments are quartered at Overcombe and John Loveday's is among them. Meanwhile many civilians have joined volunteer regiments, among them Festus Derriman, nephew of an old miser at nearby Oxwell Hall, who tries to cut a fine figure in the local 'yeomanry'. It is apparent that both John Loveday and Festus Derriman are interested in young Anne Garland.

We are offered some historical background material, such as the visit of the King (George III) to nearby Budmouth (Weymouth) and the royal review of the troops on the downs outside the town. Then Bob Loveday, the Miller's sailor son, returns from sea with a Miss Matilda Johnson, an actress whom he is intending to marry. We learn from certain signs that Anne has considered Bob at least her childhood sweetheart and that she is pained by this desertion; Bob has entirely forgotten all the feelings he might once have had for Anne.

When John Loveday meets Matilda he recognises her as an actress (she has concealed this from Bob) who has been closely involved with a number of the officers of John's regiment. John forces Matilda to leave the house secretly and give up all thought of his brother, presumably under threat of revealing her past to his family. John then explains to Bob what he has done and a coolness springs up between them: Bob sets off in search of his fiancée.

Miller Loveday and Mrs Garland are married. Anne grows cold towards John because she has heard he was seen 'courting' with a young woman (it was Matilda Johnson, whom he was, in effect, ordering to leave) so he is not unhappy when his regiment is ordered back to Exonbury. This leaves Bob and Anne together, and they soon become sweethearts, but Mrs Garland, now Mrs Loveday, is still keen to encourage the rich Festus Derriman in his attentions to Anne, so the latter's position is largely unchanged.

The announcement is now made that the French have landed and our characters prepare for battle. When Anne tries to escape inland she is separated from her companions and besieged in a cottage, not by the French but by Festus who has learnt that the announcement was a false alarm. She escapes and tells John of her treatment at the hands of Festus; John finds the swaggering yeomanry volunteer and challenges him to a duel; almost at once John sees Anne and Bob, reunited after the alarm, fall into one another's arms. He resolves to show no sign of his pain.

Bob narrowly escapes the press-gang and then decides it is his duty to join the Royal Navy to fight the French. He is accepted by Captain Hardy onto H.M.S. *Victory* and when he goes to sea (to fight in the battle of Trafalgar, among others) he tells John that he may win Anne if he can. When he returns to England he does not write to his family or visit them and eventually even John decides that his brother has lost interest in Anne and he starts to court her again. Anne is broken-hearted at Bob's second desertion and begins to turn towards the devoted John, but, just as they come closer together, Bob writes to John saying that the woman he fell in with on return from the *Victory* has proved unworthy of him and that he wishes to return to Anne. John, heroically, ends his courtship of Anne and they wait, she puzzled by John's new coolness, until Bob, now promoted Lieutenant, finally appears. With some difficulty Bob re-establishes himself in Anne's heart and John, whose regiment has been summoned to the war in Spain, departs forever. He is killed in the campaign.

Commentary

This is a fascinating novel for the student of Hardy. It is classed among the 'Romances and Fantasies' for several good reasons, but they are different from the reasons which put *A Pair of Blue Eyes* in this group. The Cornish novel has a light, satirical and self-consciously melodramatic tone more or less throughout; *The Trumpet-Major* does not share this tone, its 'romantic' element being based instead on the rural idyll that makes up a good deal of its substance and on the dramatic historical background.

Hardy was fascinated by the Napoleonic wars and spent a number of years, off and on, collecting material about them which he put to use in this novel and in *The Dynasts*. He consulted a considerable number of newspapers and periodicals of the time and he learnt a good deal, as he says himself in the Preface he wrote for the 1895 edition, from oral sources, including his grandmother. To some extent, then, this is a re-working of an accumulation of historical knowledge, and sometimes historical material seems to appear in the novel purely for its own sake and hardly with a view to advancing the plot. Thus the review of the troops on the downs near Overcombe (Chapter 12) and the meeting of Anne Garland and the King (Chapter 34) can be considered largely as historical background, romantic incidents from the history of the period.

The rural idyll, although incomplete, is clearly represented in the benevolence of nature and people manifested in Overcombe. The Miller is a kind and reliable man, his mill a venerable but attractive part of rural England; the village life around him is on the whole a matter of simple folk enjoying a quiet life. It is as if Hardy, in looking back to the year 1804, cannot resist a certain sentimentalising tendency which is the opposite of his more usual views, especially as the century advanced towards the 'future' of such characters as Little Father Time in *Jude the Obscure*. Much of the action of the novel takes place in summer, and a good deal of it in a pretty English garden.

So because of its background of rural idyll in a romantic historical setting this is a 'tale', or as its sub-title claims, a 'romance'. But that is not an adequate description, true though it may be as far as it goes. For *The Trumpet-Major* is also a Hardyesque treatise on love and fate and chance. Miller Loveday may have something in common with Tranter Dewy of *Under the Greenwood Tree* and John Loveday may be related to Dick Dewy, but the elements of chance and fate and character conspire to raise John to something of the tragic level of Michael Henchard (in *The Mayor of Casterbridge*) and Jude Fawley (in *Jude the Obscure*). Such comparisons are slightly exaggerated, but John shares with these individuals a sad death and a character which drives him into the most painful predicaments. All three are sensitive, capable of enduring pain, honourable, idealistic, a little foolish perhaps.

Anne Garland, too, is more of a character than the word 'romance' would lead us to assume. She is not merely vain or merely beautiful – indeed Hardy is at some pains to minimise these characteristics so common in his other heroines before Tess and Sue Bridehead – she is resilient and single-minded, devoted to her childhood sweetheart, sensible in her assessment of potential lovers, decent, sensitive. Between them Anne and John raise this novel to a level closer to tragedy than the rest of it would suggest. The other aspects of *The Trumpet-Major* are often impressive: the picture of Overcombe, the characterisation of its inhabitants and the historical background are handled with nothing less than brilliance. It is as if Hardy's mind starts with these more optimistic light sketches but is drawn inexorably, once love enters on the scene, towards his usual preoccupations with pain and tragedy.

Points for study

1. *Moments of ominousness*

The tragic elements in the story soon start to show through the chinks in the apparently comic narrative. Early in the novel, for instance, we read of the 'cheerful, careless, unpremeditated half-hour' when the dragoons, coming into the village to let their horses drink in the mill pond for the first time, are given cherries by the inhabitants; the scene

> returned like the scent of a flower to the memories of some of those who enjoyed it, even at a distance of many years after, when they lay wounded and weak in foreign lands (*The Trumpet-Major*, Chapter 3)

And again we briefly meet Sergeant Stanner who 'fell at the bloody battle of Albuera . . . being mortally wounded and trampled down by a French hussar'. These touches are not merely random, they indicate an undertow of tragedy beneath the surface of the novel.

2. *Set pieces*

Unlike his practice elsewhere, Hardy indulges in set-piece descriptions in this novel. Most of them are the direct result of his historical researches, for instance the descriptions of King George III at the theatre in Budmouth (Chapter 30) or of the recruits drilling so comically in anticipation of military action (Chapter 23). Some of the set pieces, however, include descriptions more typical of Hardy, the description of Oxwell Hall, for instance (Chapter 6), which is well worth analysing. Hardy himself seems conscious of these set pieces, using terms such as 'composition' to refer to the pictures he is painting (compare, for example, Chapter 15).

3. *Class*

As usual in Hardy, class differences prove to be an irritant. Fascinatingly, we are presented, in the Lovedays and the Garlands, with families who are, respectively, exactly of Hardy's own original social position and the class immediately above that. Anne and her mother are impoverished but still, just, genteel. Miller Loveday, well-respected and well-off, is not genteel. This difference looms large in Mrs Garland's consciousness, although she does eventually marry Loveday, and it still matters to the younger generation: during the scare at the time of the supposed French landing, for instance, Hardy writes:

> Anne . . . forgot the little peculiarities of speech and manner in Bob and his father, which sometimes jarred for a moment upon her more refined sense, and was thankful for their love and protection.
>
> (*The Trumpet-Major*, Chapter 25)

4. *Rustic detail*

Hardy shows even more than his usual delight in rustic and old-world detail in this novel, recalling the loving descriptions of which *Under the Greenwood Tree* is full. The preparations for Matilda Johnson's arrival at Overcombe Mill, for instance (Chapter 16), demonstrate Hardy's remarkable perceptiveness and imagination in such matters.

Two on a Tower (1882)

The Plot

Lady Constantine, aged about twenty-eight or twenty-nine, lives at the Great House in Welland, a village in South Wessex. Her husband has gone to Africa, lion-hunting, but has not returned in two years. She has promised not to indulge in any social life in his absence and her life is very dull. Then she discovers Swithin St Cleeve, a man of twenty, of an ambiguous social position (his father was a renegade curate and his mother the daughter of a farmer), using a tower on her estate as an amateur astronomical observatory. Gradually she falls in love with him, and he shows some interest in her although he is far more concerned with his science.

Swithin falls seriously ill and Lady Constantine realises how attached to him she is when she impulsively kisses him on what she takes to be his death-bed. The reader has long since become aware of the true nature of her emotions as she has taken an improbably strong interest in astronomy and has bought Swithin an expensive telescope. The young man recovers from his illness, but she wavers in her attentions to him, depending on her sense of propriety which is sometimes weaker and sometimes stronger; her love for him does not vary, nor does his ignorance of her feelings until he hears some of the local rustics discussing them. He then falls in love with her, to her pleasure but also to her confusion for, although she now has the news that her husband is long since dead and she is considerably impoverished, she is his senior still in both age and rank and does not want to interrupt his career.

Nonetheless they go away to Bath and are secretly married; and then a period of desperate concealment begins. Lady Constantine's brother, Louis, encourages her to respond to the advances of the Bishop of Melchester. Louis needs a rich husband for his sister as he is almost penniless and he sees that Lady Constantine herself had better get married soon before she is too old, she being now thirty.

Lady Constantine, of course, shows no willingness to respond to the Bishop, and Louis, made suspicious by this and by various other pieces of evidence, sets a trap to catch her and Swithin, if possible. The result is that he gets her at least to admit that she loves the young astronomer. The Bishop proposes to her by letter, but, before she has had time to send a refusal, she receives the news that her husband, although he is now indeed dead, was not in fact dead, as was reported, at the time of her marriage to Swithin which is, therefore, invalid. They decide to remarry publicly but Lady Constantine discovers that Swithin has been left a large private income on condition that he does not marry before he is twenty-five and she feels, as she felt before, that she may be standing in the way of his career. With a heroic effort she insists that he claim his legacy and she sends him off on an astronomical expedition to South Africa, saying only that they may remarry if he wishes it when he is twenty-five.

Lady Constantine then discovers that she is pregnant. She tries to catch Swithin before he sails from Southampton but just misses him. Her letters to him miscarry and, in her desperation and strongly pushed by her brother, she agrees to marry the Bishop. Swithin learns of this five months after it has happened, learns of the birth of his baby and, three years later, learns of the death of the Bishop.

He returns to England, partly because his astronomical studies at Cape Town are finished, and meets his one-time wife on the tower again. Although she no longer arouses his love (she has lost her looks) he says that he has returned to marry her as he is now twenty-five. She dies in his arms of the shock produced by this sudden happy solution.

Commentary

Hardy said that he wanted the astronomical part of this novel to be more than just background and it is easy to see why, given his usual approach to the universe. In his major novels, particularly, we have a strong sense of vast impersonal forces at work behind the scenes: Edgon Heath and its weather care little for the ant-like movements of humanity on the heath's face; Stonehenge seems to be taking, in Tess Durbeyfield, only one more victim in its long history; the long chain of chances that leads from the moment when Michael Henchard sells his wife to his final re-enactment of King Lear's scene on the heath seems to be part of a web woven by the fates. It is natural, then, that Hardy should sometimes try to bring this world view into more explicit focus; in *The Dynasts* he includes an entire celestial machinery to give us his immense perspective on the action (the Napoleonic wars) and in *Two on a Tower* he tries to relate the action to the cosmic movements of the universe as a whole.

Paradoxically this attempt seems, in its own terms at least, to be something of a failure. The descriptions of the 'Impersonal monsters, namely, Immensities' (Chapter 4) of interstellar space are marvellously done, and the romantic tragedy of Viviette Constantine and her lover makes a good story. but the two are not very closely bound together. Sometimes the action is affected by Swithin's preference for astronomy over love, but this could have been brought about by any other absorbing passion Swithin might have – chemistry or ancient history, for example. It is as if Hardy succeeded better when he merely hinted at the external depths of space, time and chance, lurking beyond the bounds of his tales; including them so explicitly destroys some of the subtlety of the novel.

Central to this, as to most of Hardy's fiction, is the passion of love, and if we have the impression that the matter of star-gazing is pushed aside by this central interest then that is perhaps not so surprising. As a tale of love *Two on a Tower* is a remarkable piece of writing. Hardy enters deeply into the feelings of a woman who falls in love with a man almost ten years her junior and he constructs a mechanism to entrap her that gives him a lot of scope for psychological and sociological analysis. He considers the influence of relative ages on love; the role of class; the effect of concealment; the question of what constitutes a true marriage; the effect of love on a promising scientific career; the desirability of marriage in difficult circumstances; what effect the wishes of a distant, or dead, husband should have on a woman; the debt, if any, which a woman owes to her older brother, and the relationship between love and religious devotion.

The novel is, in other words, a mine of Hardy's views and opinions, and it has the usual structure of his fiction (a woman hemmed in by circumstances and besieged by men) but it includes an even wider range of topics than the other novels and is well worth studying for these reasons.

Points for study

---

1. *The universe*

It comes as no surprise to the student of Hardy that prolonged study of the universe is hardly likely to have a cheerful effect. Swithin, in his very first conversation with Lady Constantine, says that he wants to become the Astronomer Royal 'If I live. Perhaps I shall not live.' A few sentences further on he comments 'Time is short, and science is infinite – how infinite only those who study astronomy realise – and perhaps I shall be worn out before I make my mark.' Hardy then says of Lady Constantine:

> She seemed to be greatly struck by the odd mixture in him of scientific earnestness and melancholy mistrust of all things human. Perhaps it was owing to the nature of his studies.
>
> (*Two on a Tower*, Chapter 1)

Too much study of the universe produces gloom. This view is juxtaposed with the view of 'Haymoss' Fry, the rustic labourer who says to Lady Constantine, just after her first interview with Swithin, something about 'Master God' and goes on: 'But be dazed if I believe in such trumpery about folks in the sky, nor anything else that's said on them, good or bad.' (*Two on a Tower*, Chapter 1). This almost blasphemous opinion (Fry's 'dazed' is a euphemism for 'damned') with its strident atheistic tone makes an interesting contrast with Swithin's view of what is in the 'sky'.

2. *Man*

There is a similar counterpoint between astronomy and the rustic view over the matter of mankind. Hezekiah Biles, 'Haymoss' and the others agree that if they had 'the making of labouring men for a twelvemonth' they would make a better job of it than God, in particular increasing man's strength (Chapter 2). Swithin tells Lady Constantine that 'whatever the stars were made for, they were not made to please our eyes. It is just the same in everything; nothing is made for man' (Chapter 4).

3. *A chapter of introspection*

Chapter 35 of *Two on a Tower* repays attention. It consists almost entirely of Lady Constantine's weighing up of the moral, social and practical consequences that may follow from her complicated legal and emotional position. As usual with Hardy, the noble impulses carry the day at the end of this piece of painful introspection, and she decides to release Swithin from his obligations to her in order that he may pursue his career. Generosity is more common in Hardy than in many Victorian novelists.

4. *Some Hardyesque motifs*

Hardy returns several times in his fiction to a series of intriguing and instructive motifs. In this novel we meet, among others:

1. The Ten Commandments (Chapter 11) – compare the scene in *Jude the Obscure* where Sue and Jude have to paint the decalogue during a church restoration
2. Previous generations buried beneath us (Chapter 18) – compare the Roman legionaries buried in and near Casterbridge in *The Mayor of Casterbridge*
3. Weddings as funerals (Chapter 19) – compare Widow Edlin's comment at the end of *Jude the Obscure*, 'weddings be funerals nowadays'

The Well-Beloved (1897)

The plot

Jocelyn Pierston returns to the 'Isle of Slingers' (Portland), his native place, after some years trying to become a sculptor in London. He meets again his childhood sweetheart, Avice Caro, and proposes to her, but it is clear that he only sees her as the temporary incarnation of his elusive romantic ideal – 'the Well-Beloved', a spirit of womanhood which he sees embodied in one real woman after another. This is borne out when, on impulse, Pierston travels to London with an attractive young woman from the Island who has run away from her father, and proposes to marry her instead. On the train journey he has realised that she is the Well-Beloved now.

Pierston and this new incarnation, Marcia Bencomb, spend some days together in a London hotel during which she decides to return to her father rather than marry her sculptor. When she does so she is taken on a tour round the world and Avice Caro, meanwhile, has married a cousin. Pierston returns to his sculpture and lives as a bachelor, falling in love with various manifestations of the Well-Beloved from time to time but not pursuing the woman in question lest the divine touch in her be destroyed by familiarity.

When he is about forty Pierston meets a Mrs Pine-Avon, a recent widow, at a party. It seems as if she is to be the latest Well-Beloved but Pierston receives a letter from the Island in which he learns that Avice Caro, whom he has not seen for twenty years, is dead. Although he has long since decided that his ideal was never incarnated in her while she was alive he finds himself to be passionately in love with her now that she is dead. He returns to the Island on the day of her funeral and, having visited her grave, calls at her house which is now occupied only by her daughter. This girl is about nineteen and is almost the double of her mother at the time of her engagement to Pierston. She too, bears the names Avice and Caro (although she is also 'Ann') and she is best thought of as Avice II. She is more down-to-earth than her mother, a poor laundrywoman in fact, while Pierston is now rich and famous.

He rents a large house, close to Avice II's cottage, for two or three months and strikes up an acquaintance with her although the contrast in their positions is rather embarrassing. She confesses to him that she too can only fall in love for short periods, and that she has already been in love fifteen times, but he resolves to marry her in spite of everything. It seems, however, that she is quite indifferent to him and has a lover of her own. Without explaining her reasons she says she must get away from the Island and Pierston takes her to his flat in London where she becomes his only servant. He proposes to her and, although she seems to have softened towards him somewhat, she refuses him. It is then revealed that she is married to a fellow islander, Isaac, whom she does not like, and who has gone to Guernsey. Pierston takes Avice II back to the Island and summons Isaac, who arrives just in time to discover that he is the father of a baby daughter. Pierston returns to London to find that Nichola Pine-Avon is about to marry his friend Somers.

Twenty years pass. Pierston visits the Island again and becomes friendly with Avice II (now a widow) but falls in love with her daughter, the more educated and elegant Avice III, now about twenty. He tells her mother that he is interested in this new incarnation of the Well-Beloved and she thinks favourably of the suit, indeed it turns out that she has written and asked him to visit the Island for just this purpose. Avice III is rather put off by Pierston's age but she agrees to marry him to please her mother, who is ill, and she is even able to accept him after hearing that he has loved her mother and her grandmother. But her heart is really given to a young man from Jersey and, when she sees him for what is meant to be the last time she decides to run away with him instead. The shock kills Avice II, who has a weak heart. Pierston, sitting by her corpse in her house (his old house) is visited by the mother of the young man with whom Avice III has run away – it turns out to be Marcia Bencomb from forty years before. They become friends, settle on the Island and eventually marry. Pierston loses his artistic gift and his obsession with the Well-Beloved simultaneously.

Commentary

The Well-Beloved, written before *Jude the Obscure* and rewritten after the publication of that novel, shares with it a 'geometrical' form. Hardy used that word to describe the plot of *Jude* and, at the end of *The Well-Beloved*, when Pierston and Marcia's neighbours express the wish that they should be married, Hardy talks of this as a wish 'to give a geometrical shape to their story' (Part 3, Chapter 8). It is a schematic novel which explores the emotion of erotic love almost exclusively from the point of view of the hero: he is an artist 'cursed' with a devotion to an elusive beauty that can appear in improbable women and disappear suddenly. There are distinct similarities between Jocelyn Pierston, the hero, and Hardy himself, as is borne out by the poem which opens 'I look into my glass'.

The scheme of the novel is intended to demonstrate various Hardyesque theses about love: love is like an affliction, a doom laid on men by a cruel goddess; love is not altogether rational and has more to do with the fantasies of the lover than with the real qualities of the beloved; love can ruin a man's life or at least make a fool of him. In addition to these Hardy adds something new, something probably highly autobiographical: love is closely associated with artistic inspiration. Pierston's 'curse' seems to have two sides, his sculpting, in which he often attempts the likeness of Aphrodite and other goddesses of love, and love itself, which attracts him so powerfully to one woman or another. These two things are closely linked and, specifically, when the artistic muse abandons Pierston, so does his capacity for love (Part 3, Chapter 8).

As in the other novels, love is not a source of much happiness. There is a strong suggestion that it is something which comes and goes according to unfathomable laws and that unless it is grabbed when it first appears it will wither; thus Pierston abandons Avice I once he has got to know her thoroughly, Marcia Bencomb abandons Pierston once they have spent a few days together, Isaac abandons Avice II shortly after their marriage and Avice III tries to leave her husband when they have been married for less than a year. These are only some of the examples in the novel of the first flush of love not surviving protracted contact. Love, infuriatingly , seems to thrive where it is rendered impossible, as in the case of the death of Avice I which arouses Pierston to a new height of infatuation:

> He loved the woman dead and inaccessible as he had never loved her in life . . . the times of youthful friendship with her . . . flamed up into a yearning and passionate attachment.
>
> (*The Well-Beloved,* Part 2, Chapter 3)

This seems remarkably prophetic of the emotions Hardy was to feel after the death of his first wife (see 'Poems 1912-1913').

Behind all this predictable commentary on the unsatisfactory nature of love, and of life, stands, as usual, a thoroughly realised landscape – the 'Isle of Slingers'. This is not merely scenery – as always in Hardy it is explored for its associations, its history, its peculiarities, its power. The Island is old, Roman, even Celtic, isolated and inward-looking, with its own traditions and dialect and these Hardy uses as part of his tale. The ominous seashore and the dangerous weather play their parts in creating the unsettling atmosphere of the novel.

Points for study

1. *The goddess*

Hardy starts from the idea that there was a Roman temple to Venus on the Island and underpins his novel with references to this goddess of love (Aphrodite to the Greeks) and to her other incarnations such as Astarte and Freya. As a son of the Island Pierston seems to be a natural worshipper of this dangerous divinity and he comes to feel that he is being tormented by her for not having remained faithful to his first Island love – Avice I. At times it seems as if it is the goddess herself who appears as the 'Well-Beloved', as though the glimpses of the ideal which Pierston catches in various women are in fact glimpses of Venus herself. References to this goddess appear in Part 1, Chapter 2; Part 2, Chapter 3; Part 2, Chapter 5; Part 2, Chapter 6; Part 2, Chapter 9; Part 2, Chapter 12 and Part 3, Chapter 2. This last reference is perhaps the most interesting.

2. *Ambition*
Pierston's ambition (achieved) to become a Royal Academician parallels to some extent Swithin St Cleeve's ambition to become the Astronomer Royal (in *Two on a Tower*) and Jude Fawley's ambition to become a Doctor of Divinity (in *Jude the Obscure*), both of which of course remain unfulfilled.

3. *Inheritance*
Hardy was a Darwinist and interested in inherited characteristics. In this novel he stresses the inbred nature of the Islanders who reveal features of a supposed Roman ancestry. In the shorter term he considers the genetic relationship between the three Avices rather carefully. See, for instance, Part 2, Chapter 12, particularly the paragraph opening 'At sight of her . . .'.

4. *Romance*
This novel has the lightness of touch of the 'Romances and Fantasies' among which it is numbered but the ideas it plays with, however lightly, are clearly serious at heart. Perhaps Hardy used this general title in a special and personal way; it would be worth enquiring exactly what he meant, particularly, by 'fantasy'.

5. *Poem*
See the poem 'The Well-Beloved' in *Poems of the Past and the Present*.

Chapter 6

'Novels of Ingenuity'

Desperate Remedies (1871)

The plot

Cytherea Graye and her brother Owen are left impoverished orphans by the death of their architect father. They move to Budmouth on the Wessex coast and Owen works in an architect's office where the head draughtsman is Edward Springrove; Cytherea and Edward fall in love but Edward goes to London to pursue his vocation. Cytherea offers herself as a lady's maid and her advertisement is answered by a Miss Aldclyffe of Knapwater House; when Cytherea starts work at Knapwater she discovers that Miss Aldclyffe is the same young woman who once jilted her father, and left him heartbroken, for reasons he was never able to discover. She is now nearly fifty and a bad-tempered and lonely spinster.

Miss Aldclyffe advertises for an architect-cum-steward for her estate, necessary now that her old father has died. She hires Aeneas Manston and rejects Edward even though his father, also Edward Springrove, is the landlord of the inn near Knapwater. Cytherea discovers that Edward, the son, is engaged to be married to a local young woman, his cousin, and, tearfully, she writes to tell him that all is therefore over between them. Meanwhile it becomes apparent that Manston is passionately in love with her. This is awkward as Manston is married to an actress, whom he does not love, and things become more awkward when his wife writes to Miss Aldclyffe and persuades her, under threat of revealing something about her past, to effect a reunion between her and her husband. Miss Aldclyffe does this by insisting that Manston bring his wife to live with him and he writes to her asking her to come down from London.

By a simple mistake Manston fails to meet his wife, and she goes to old Mr Springrove's inn to spend the night. A fire starts, accidentally, which consumes the inn and some neighbouring cottages and kills Mrs Manston. Young Edward Springrove has also come down from London to visit his father and the two rivals for Cytherea's love now meet. Manston, who, we are being told obliquely, is Miss Aldclyffe's illegitimate son, asks her to ensure that Springrove marries his cousin so that Cytherea can be his. The destruction of the cottages has put old Mr Springrove in Miss Aldclyffe's power to the extent of her being able to insist that he rebuild them at his expense: Manston forces his mother to insist on her rights in this respect while offering to waive them if Edward marries his cousin. This he reluctantly agrees to do in order to save his father's financial position and even his sanity. Cytherea is heart-broken.

Gradually Manston starts to court Cytherea. She is cold towards him until her brother falls ill, effectively loses his job and needs an operation and financial help. Miss Aldclyffe and Manston offer this help, on condition that Cytherea accepts Manston. Eventually she agrees to marry him. On the day of their wedding Edward learns that his cousin has jilted him and has married a rich neighbouring farmer, but it is too late, and Manston and Cytherea are married. Then it is discovered that Manston's former wife may not after all have perished in the fire at the inn. Owen and Edward pursue Manston and Cytherea to Southampton and manage to separate them just in time. Mrs Manston then reappears and takes up her abode with Manston amid rumours of deceit, collusion and bigamy. Edward proposes to Cytherea, who refuses him because of the gossip about what happened on her wedding evening in Southampton.

Owen and Edward now engage in some detective work which reveals, in spite of Manston's attempts to conceal it, that the 'Mrs Manston' now living with him is not the same person as the Mrs Manston who pretended she had been killed in the fire. Manston's motive in substituting this woman for the other, and what Cytherea's real position therefore is, now become the main centres of interest. It turns out that Manston has murdered his first wife, on discovering that she escaped from the fire, and has chosen to pretend that she is still alive (thereby losing Cytherea) rather than encourage enquiry into her whereabouts. In trying to shift her body to a more secure burial-place Manston is spied on by a policeman, warned by the Rector, Mr Raunham, and by the substitute 'Mrs Manston'. He is apprehended and hangs himself in gaol, thus leaving Cytherea free. Miss Aldclyffe dies, partly from the shock of her son's death, and leaves Knapwater House, effectively, to Cytherea and Edward, who are married.

Commentary

Hardy's first published novel, *Desperate Remedies* contains several elements of interest to the student. He had been advised to produce something 'sensational' and this he did: in the later chapters, particularly, sensation, suspense and melodrama pile up with a vengeance in the mode of Dickens and Wilkie Collins (1824-89), the virtual creator of the detective story. This tendency reaches its peak in Chapter 19 when the substitute 'Mrs Manston' is watching the detective who is following Miss Aldclyffe who is trailing Manston who is in the process of re-burying his murdered wife's body at the dead of night. This sort of thing may appear overdone but it must have served as an apprenticeship in the ordering of coincidences at which Hardy was to become so expert. Even in this novel some of the machinery of the plot is skilfully worked out; for example the discovery that the substitute 'Mrs Manston' is different from the real Mrs Manston is initiated by the reading of a poem of Manston's that Edward Springrove has tracked down in which he calls his wife's eyes 'azure' while the substitute's eyes are black; best of all, however, is the fact that it is the woman, Cytherea, who, typically, notices the discrepancy.

Even in this first novel, too, Hardy shows his remarkable skill at handling the dialogue of his rustics. Clerk Crickett, Gad Weedy and the others are worthy predecessors to the 'rustic choruses' of the later novels and their dialogue is impressive. The final chapter of the story, 'Sequel', is a description by these rustics of Edward and Cytherea's wedding and its circumstances: all that we have waited so long to hear about the happiness of the young couple thus comes to us obliquely through the mouths of these lesser mortals. It is a successful move on Hardy's part, though not one he was to use extensively later.

If we leave aside the sensational and melodramatic elements (which dominate the novel after Chapter 13 but not really before) we have the ingredients of a 'normal' Hardy novel. Besides the rustics we have a description of village life, of the lady at the big house, of love between people who are struggling on the margins between the classes and of the way circumstances conspire against human happiness. For all that has been said against it, *Desperate Remedies* could only have been written by Hardy: we can identify his hand in every paragraph.

Points for study

1. *Self-portrait*
There is reason to assume that Edward Springrove, Junior, is something of a self-portrait by Hardy. Certainly they share a profession, a class status, something of their appearance and an inclination to write verse that will not be published. See, for example, Chapter 2, Section 3.

2. *Lesbianism?*
In Chapter 6, Section 1, Miss Aldclyffe and Cytherea are in bed together. One feels that in a novel published in mid-Victorian England

Hardy cannot have been suggesting a sexual relationship, but his vocabulary tends strongly that way and it may be significant that he toned it down in later revisions. At all events, there is only a thin line dividing the sexual and non-sexual actions of a person as 'passionate' as Miss Aldclyffe.

3. *Virgil*
One of the first books Hardy was given was the seventeenth-century English translation, by John Dryden (1631-1700), of the *Aeneid*, the great Latin epic by Virgil (70-19BC). It seems that this was in his mind when he wrote *Desperate Remedies*. 'Cytherea' is a name for Venus whose son, Aeneas, is the hero of Virgil's epic: in Hardy *Cytherea* Aldclyffe turns out to be the mother of *Aeneas* Manston. Besides these allusions there are half a dozen quotations from the Latin poet in the novel. Is Hardy doing any more than wearing his learning on his sleeve?

4. *Chapter 10*
Hardy's capacity for handling dramatic events is already well developed. Here the way in which developments run together towards the tragic climax of the fire is beautifully paced. We can compare this chapter with the events leading up to the death of Troy in *Far From the Madding Crowd*.

The Hand of Ethelberta (1876)

The plot

Ethelberta Petherwin, née Chickerel, is the young widow of a young man of upper-class connexions although she is herself only from the servant class. At Anglebury in South Wessex she meets by chance a former suitor of hers, the somewhat impoverished music teacher Christopher Julian who lives quietly with his sister. Soon afterwards Julian also meets Picotee, Ethelberta's younger sister, and it becomes apparent that both of these young women are attracted to him. Ethelberta sends him, anonymously, a volume of her own verse and Julian's old love for her is rekindled.

The scene shifts to London. Here, at a fashionable dinner-party, we meet Mr Ladywell, Mr Neigh and a butler called Chickerel who turns out to be the father of Ethelberta, Picotee and several other children. Ethelberta's poems are the talk of the town, and when she falls out with her rich mother-in-law she decides to make the most of her literary talents by becoming a professional story-teller in London. She is such a success at this that she is soon able to establish herself in a smart house with most of her family as servants. Her brothers Sol and Dan have come to London from Wessex, too, and they repair and decorate the house for her. Picotee follows them in her anxiety to see something of Julian (who has also come to London) with whom she is now very much in love.

Julian, however, continues faithful to Ethelberta, in spite of Mr Ladywell's obvious attentions to her, and Ethelberta announces that she will marry him when he becomes richer. He can do no better than get a job as an assistant organist at Melchester cathedral and, when Ethelberta's story-telling begins to lose popularity, she considers taking up Mr Neigh's offer to marry her in order to support her family. The elderly Lord Mountclere also pays his attentions to her, so now she has three London suitors as well as Julian at Melchester in Wessex. At this juncture Ethelberta takes her family to Knollsea for a holiday on the Wessex coast. Here she finds herself in an awkward position between her own class and that of her friends and patrons when she meets Lord Mountclere and some other aristocrats and Mr Neigh.

Both Lord Mountclere and Mr Neigh now follow Ethelberta across the Channel to Rouen and Mr Ladywell joins her there, too, so all her well-to-do lovers are around her again. The news that she is a butler's daughter has begun to circulate in London, and she feels she had better marry someone before it is too late. But Neigh and Ladywell overhear Lord Mountclere proposing to her and it looks as if her scheme may fail; his lordship does propose unreservedly but she cannot decide whether to accept him or not and returns to England. There she reveals her family connexions to Lord Mountclere and he, who had discovered them already, persists in his proposal of marriage, which she accepts. To test whether she is still in love with Julian Lord Mountclere takes Ethelberta to Melchester where the signs of love are apparent enough but where Picotee can be passed off as the victim, as indeed she is.

When it becomes known that Ethelberta is about to marry Lord Mountclere, the peer's brother sets out with Ethelberta's brother to try to prevent the match, the former anxious about the future of the title (which would pass to him if his brother had no heir) and the latter concerned about what has been heard of Lord Mountclere's character. Julian also decides to visit Ethelberta to tell her of her prospective husband's undesirability and these three arrive in South Wessex on the morning of the wedding day, as does Ethelberta's father. All four converge on her residence at Knollsea but it is too late as she has married the old peer. Ethelberta attempts to leave Lord Mountclere when she discovers that he has recently kept a mistress, but becomes reconciled to him and indeed comes to dominate their marriage. Julian goes away to Italy but, on his return, proposes to and is accepted by Picotee.

Commentary

This novel, subtitled 'A Comedy in Chapters' avoids the tragic gloom which pervades much of Hardy's other work. There are no deaths, which puts it alongside *Under the Greenwood Tree* and makes it something of a rarity among Hardy's novels, and if the love between the hero and heroine is never fulfilled it is portrayed as less passionate and painful than love usually is for Hardy's major characters. On the other hand the novel does focus on some of its author's central obsessions: marriage, class and the nature of woman.

As its title implies, *The Hand of Ethelberta* is concerned with who will marry the heroine and why. She has exceptionally numerous suitors for a Hardy heroine (four, plus two brothers and a father who have views as to the disposal of her hand) and it is implied that in London she has probably made a number of other conquests too. The story builds up through a series of episodes that all increase the tension surrounding the question of her marriage. She quickly realises that the only route to social and financial salvation for herself and her family will be through marriage. The last quarter of the book, in particular, is taken up entirely with the pursuit of Ethelberta by her lovers. They follow her to Rouen and to Knollsea and the story is driven forward by the manoeuvres of both lovers and family with regard to her marriage: if she marries whose heart will be broken? What will become of her family? What will happen to Lord Mounclere's heir and brother? What will become of Lord Mountclere himself, of Ethelberta herself? These questions are resolved by resorting to a number of familiar Hardy stratagems surrounding marriage: the pursuit/flight in difficult weather, the church where the wedding has taken place, the horrified lover who is an onlooker at the ceremony, the desperate attempt to prevent consummation. If weddings are a ritualised dance that precedes mating Hardy extends the ritual and lingers over its details in a delaying tactic of great psychological interest.

As to class, in this novel we have the usual poor-man-and-lady theme complicated by the fact that the 'lady' herself is of the servant class and that it is she who marries the richest and most aristocratic of her suitors. Sol, Ethelberta's brother, is a republican socialist and we are offered almost the full range of class strata in the novel, with an emphasis on the top and bottom of the scale. This almost Dickensian scope extends to the geography of the novel, too, and we are hustled about from Wessex cottages to London mansions, stately homes and even to France. Perhaps this becomes a weakness when we compare it with the intense concentration on one limited area that marks Hardy's best work such as *The Return of the Native* and *The Woodlanders*.

Ethelberta is really another of Hardy's feminist heroines. She is highly talented, a natural leader and certainly the most powerful member of her family. She shows how a woman can take her fate into her own hands just as much as a man. And yet Ethelberta is, as they say, all woman. She is passionate, anxious and peremptory as well as steady, clever and sensible. Like Tess she looks after her brothers and sisters (see Chapter 13, for instance). Perhaps she is in some ways a self-portrait by Hardy: she raises herself into the upper class by means of her talent for telling stories in something of the way he did, and her first step is a marriage above her station, as his was. She is even conscious, as Hardy was, of the discrepancy between what a writer says and what he feels and of the dangers of self-revelation. Julian says of her, for instance, 'People who print very warm words have sometimes cold manners' (Chapter 2).

Points for study

1. *Chapter 1*
This chapter has in it some good comic dialogue between rustics and a remarkable scene in which Ethelberta watches a duck ingeniously avoiding the pursuit of a hawk. But are these elements ever integrated into the narrative which follows, as they are in his greater novels? There is no real 'rustic chorus' here and the bird symbolism is not developed.

2. *Satire*
Hardy refers in *The Hand of Ethelberta* to the 'satire of circumstances' (Chapter 13), as opposed to satire 'in words', and the novel is satirical in both senses. Here as always Hardy is conscious of the tricks played on men by mere chance and circumstance, and he does a little satirising himself, particularly in the London scenes of the novel. London always made Hardy adopt a rather harsh and brittle satirical tone, as in *A Pair of Blue Eyes*, for example.

3. *Power*
The novel shows, more clearly than most others, Hardy's view of the *balance* of power between the sexes: Mr Neigh has power over Ethelberta, for instance, when he states that he will marry her and she at once becomes over-excited, but we also see her exercising her power in rejecting Mr Ladywell, and her domination over Lord Mountclere.

4. *Servants*
Hardy was aware that some of his ancestors in his mother's side were servants and he was very interested in domestic service. In this novel

we find some of the bitterness of servants (Sol Chickerel, Menlove), their humour (Joey and the antics of Chapter 29) and their dignity (old Mr Chickerel, content with his life as a butler).

A Laodicean (1881)

The plot

George Somerset, an independent-minded young architect, visits Stancy Castle in Outer Wessex (Somerset) and meets its owner, Miss Paula Power, after hearing a great deal about her from her companion and from the landlord at the inn at the village of Sleeping-Green. The companion is a Miss Charlotte de Stancy whose father, Sir William de Stancy, lives in a small house near the great castle he once owned, which is now Paula's residence. Before meeting Paula, too, we encounter a slightly alarming young man by the name of William Dare.

Paula has been left the castle by her father, who made a fortune building railways, and she is 'modern' in her delight in new inventions, but she is also captivated by the medieval beauty of her home and is seriously involved in stale theological disputes with the local Baptist minister by whom she cannot bring herself to be baptised. She decides to restore the castle and asks Somerset to undertake the work, which he does with the assistance of William Dare, who turns out to be too lazy to be Somerset's assistant for long. The architect finds that his growing love for Paula is perhaps matched by a similar emotion on her part and the first part of the novel ('Book the First') ends on a note of optimism.

'Book the Second' opens with a plot hatched between Dare and a local architect, Havill. Somerset has insisted that Havill be given an opportunity to compete for the architectural work at the castle and Havill and Dare, the latter for reasons as yet unexplained, steal copies of Somerset's designs for the competition. There now appears on the scene Captain de Stancy, son of Sir William, brother of Charlotte and, to our surprise, father of the illegitimate Dare. Dare, infinitely more cunning than his father, has decided to attempt a match between Captain de Stancy and Paula in order to restore his family's fortunes and with them his own. He arouses his father's interest by showing him Paula doing exercises in her gymnasium in an enticing costume.

'Book the Third' concerns de Stancy's wooing of Paula. He gains her good opinion by suggesting that she should allow Havill, who has fallen on hard times, to execute the first part of the architectural work, leaving the second part, perhaps a year later, to Somerset. He also has the romantic advantage of being a de Stancy, and he has Dare to help him. But Havill's conscience gets the better of him and he resigns from the architectural work leaving the field open for Somerset who is thus thrown into direct competition with Captain de Stancy. An uncle of Paula's now appears after a ten-year absence and he, too, takes de Stancy's side and, indeed, takes her away to Nice for a long stay while Somerset is left working on the castle. Paula has still not told Somerset clearly that she loves him.

'Book the Fourth' opens with an exchange of letters and telegraph messages between Nice and Castle Stancy. Paula is 'tantalizing' Somerset in her delays and in her refusal to give him a firm answer. After a long silence from her Somerset makes his way to the South of France whither, he learns, Captain de Stancy has preceded him. There are some complicated developments between Paula, de Stancy and Dare, who has turned up in his Mephistophelean manner, and Somerset's chances appear to be diminishing.

'Book the Fifth' opens in Strasbourg. Here de Stancy's suit seems to prosper and he accompanies Paula and her relations from the city to Baden and other places in Germany. At Carlsruhe they are once more overtaken by Somerset and Dare. The former has fallen from Paula's favour as a result of Dare's trickery and is dismissed, but Paula cannot bring herself to forget him or, finally, to accept de Stancy. When eventually she does accept him events move so that she learns of his true relationship with Dare only on their wedding morning. She then turns down de Stancy finally.

In 'Book the Sixth' Paula pursues Somerset round Normandy and eventually catches him and tells him that he may marry her if he will. They marry at once and when they return to Wessex it is just in time to watch Stancy Castle being burned to the ground. The Mephistopheles, Dare, is of course the arsonist.

Commentary

Often seen as Hardy's weakest novel, *A Laodicean* is still a great deal more interesting than most minor Victorian fiction. For the student of Hardy, especially, it reveals some of its author's concerns with unusual clarity. It is based, like so many of his novels, on the 'Poor man and the Lady' theme. Somerset is not actually poor (his father is a successful painter) but Paula Power is immensely rich and lives in a large castle where she seems more like a queen or a princess than a mere 'Lady' so the relative positions of lover and beloved are maintained. Of course, Somerset, like Stephen Smith in *A Pair of Blue Eyes*, is an architect and Hardy indulges in a young architect's day-dream in allowing him a huge and fascinating restoration project on a virtually unlimited budget.

Yet there is something amiss in this fairy-tale. First, Paula is not really, strictly speaking, a 'Lady' at all, let alone a queen: she is the daughter not of an aristocrat but of a self-made engineer. The relationship between this aspect of her and her fascination with the de Stancy family gives us a remarkable insight into the Victorian mind in general and Hardy's mind in particular. In this novel he allows the present to meet the past with a vengeance: while restoring a medieval castle Paula uses the latest technological invention, the electric telegraph, and it is in her capacity as a thoroughly 'modern' young woman, exercising in her gymnasium, that she captures the heart of the last of the old de Stancy line, Captain de Stancy. The tension between ancient and modern is so strong that it comes almost as a relief when Dare burns down the castle at the end of the novel – we notice that he carefully collects all the heirlooms and family portraits he can find with which to start the fire.

The Victorian confusion of identity, epitomised by Paula's bourgeois desire to have 'romantic and historical' ancestors of 'another sort' to those she possesses (Chapter 14), is completed by her bold and amazing claim that she is 'Greek': 'I am Greek' she says (Chapter 10). Here the Victorian romantic longing for a different, older and supposedly purer world is quite unmistakable.

Once all this is established, however, and we have identified the tensions in the novel, Hardy's grip on the plot seems to slacken. The second half of the book is filled with complicated and rather purposeless wanderings about Europe. First Somerset and then Paula narrowly miss catching up with each other so often that the effect becomes comic and the final feeling we are left with is a certain relief that the hero and heroine can at last be left in peace.

Points for study

1. *The title*

A 'Laodicean' is one who is lukewarm in religion, neither hot nor cold. Paula suffers from this lukewarmness as far as becoming a full member of the Baptist church is concerned. But the title seems also to apply to the state of her heart. She loves Somerset but perhaps not with sufficient passion; after all, she is, in today's terms, a multi-millionairess, with only a vague uncle to control her lightly. Hardy carefully prevents her from admitting, to Somerset or to herself, that she loves him until the final book. Perhaps she is a Laodicean lover, too.

2. *Delay*

Unusually for Hardy, he delays introducing Paula to the reader for six whole chapters at the start of the novel. It is as if he is primarily intrigued by the architect and the castle and almost as if Paula is merely a necessary adjunct to these. This heightens the impression of her remoteness and her queen-like quality but it also allows her to appear more passive than she would be if she had burst upon us at the outset.

3. *Watching*
In most of Hardy's novels men spy cn and watch the heroine. Seeing unseen seems an essential ingredient in love and in other human relationships in the world of Wessex. The high point of this mild obsession of Hardy's surely comes in this novel, in Book 2, Chapter 7, where Dare watches Captain de Stancy watching Paula through a chink in her gymnasium wall. She is doing exercises on a swing, and is in a state of undress that at once captures the Captain's heart, as Dare knows it will. There is something here of the excitement for a male author of entering, even if only in imagination, the secret world of the Victorian lady, a penetration into a forbidden sanctum that says something about Hardy's own psychology.

4. *Autobiography*
Hardy was ill while writing the greater part of *A Laodicean*, and he drew on his memories of his own honeymoon trip to Europe for much of the somewhat unnecessary material of Books 5 and 6. Sometimes these books almost descend to the level of mere travelogues, as though Hardy is simply copying from his travel notes. More important, perhaps, are the autobiographical elements in the characters of Paula's two suitors. Somerset is the idealised young architect with the luck that Hardy would no doubt have liked to have and de Stancy is Hardyesque in one more significant way: he is profoundly susceptible to women and knows that unless he makes an enormous effort he will fall in love with every beauty he sees. Hardy himself never grew out of his own strong susceptibility in this direction.

Chapter 7

The short stories

BECAUSE OF HIS ACHIEVEMENTS as a poet and novelist, it is sometimes easy to forget that Hardy was a first-class short-story writer. He took his stories seriously, as is evidenced by the inclusion of *Wessex Tales* (1888) and *Life's Little Ironies* (1894) among his 'Novels of Character and Environment'. *A Group of Noble Dames* (1891) he placed in the category of 'Romances and Fantasies' and for *A Changed Man and Other Tales* (1913) he created a special category, 'Mixed Novels'. These four volumes, containing in all forty-five tales, put Hardy into something of the same category as D.H. Lawrence, who was also a novelist and a poet and who also published some fifty stories. The best of the Hardy stories, too, put him alongside the masters of the genre, Maupassant, Chekhov, 'Saki' and Kipling. The following account of the stories concentrates upon those that are likely to be the most profitable for a student of Hardy to read.

The stories range from the slight and the curious to the moving and thought-provoking. Hardy was always interested in the macabre and the coincidental and he remembered from his childhood many of the fireside stories of Wessex that dwelt on these aspects of life. Some of his tales are, indeed, reworkings of old and perhaps true stories, as the title of one of them ('A Tradition of Eighteen Hundred and Four') makes plain. In the Preface to *Wessex Tales* it is obvious that he is more concerned with this antiquarian and traditional aspect than with the more purely literary features of this work. He apologises for including two stories of hangmen and one of a military execution in the collection, but excuses himself by observing that 'In the neighbourhood of county-towns hanging matters used to form a large proportion of the local tradition' (*Wessex Tales*, Preface). In other words, these are tales taken, if not from the life, then from people for whom they were true stories, a 'local tradition'. Nearly all the stories include a narrator, 'old Solomon Selby', 'the old gentleman', 'the land-surveyor, my authority for the particulars of this story', and so on. These narrators may themselves be fictional but they indicate Hardy's consciousness of the oral tradition to which he was indebted. They give the stories a historical flavour, put them into a frame as it were, indicating perhaps that they are not to be taken quite as seriously as the novels. And in general the content of the stories bears this out; they tend to be set well before Hardy's own day and to contain comic, bizarre and somewhat macabre material which has survived so long on account of its strange, coincidental or unnatural character.

Thus *A Group of Noble Dames* can truly be said to be one of the 'Romances and Fantasies'. All the stories in it, except possibly the last which is ambiguous, are told by identified members of the South-Wessex Field and Antiquarian Club and concern the doings of aristocratic ladies of the seventeenth and eighteenth centuries. They involve love and matrimonial tangles which take place at such times as the Civil War of the 1640s, when such matters were more than usually difficult to carry out. The best of these is perhaps 'Barbara of the House of Grebe' in which the heroine keeps a statue of her first husband in a closet in her bedroom; her second husband, determined to win her love away from this marble Adonis, has the statue disfigured in just the same way that its original was, towards the end of his life, by a fire. His wife then becomes utterly devoted to him and quite rejects all memories of her first love. This triangle of love, with its jealousy and pain and with the curious fetishism of the statue of the beloved, anticipates motifs from Hardy's major fiction. The story is satisfying and memorable even if, like all the others in this collection, it is told with a lightness of touch that prevents us from taking it fully seriously.

Life's Little Ironies includes 'A Few Crusted Characters' which is in itself a collection of loosely connected anecdotes of a light kind. 'Absentmindedness In A Parish Choir', for instance, is a story, three pages or so in length, about a 'Quire', very similar to that of *Under The Greenwood Tree*, who all fall asleep in the church gallery under the influence of drink and when they wake up, rather confused, instead of giving out a hymn-tune they start playing a jig called 'The Devil Among the Tailors' for which transgression they are replaced with an organ.

Life's Little Ironies also contains some more substantial stories, notably 'An Imaginative Woman' which tells of a woman falling in love with a poet whom she has never met. Instead, she spends some time on holiday staying in his rooms in a lodging-house at Solentsea on the Upper Wessex coast. Through hearing about him, living in his rooms, seeing his photograph and reading his poems she becomes infatuated with him and when he commits suicide, partly out of sheer loneliness, she bitterly regrets not having contacted him. When she herself dies, in childbirth, she leaves her husband with four children; two years later her husband notices the youngest child's likeness to the photograph of the poet which he has found and, calculating the dates, concludes wrongly that the child is the product of an affair his wife must have had with a man she never even met.

'A Tragedy of Two Ambitions' tells of two curates, brothers, who allow their father to drown rather than risk his spoiling the ambitious marriage they have arranged for their sister. The Fiddler of the Reels' is a story of hypnotism and the influence of music and of faintly diabolic power exercised by the sinister violinist Wat Ollamoor over women. These are the most significant stories in the volume.

In *Wessex Tales* all seven stories are of interest but the most remarkable three are 'The Three Strangers', 'The Withered Arm' and 'The Distracted Preacher'. 'The Three Strangers' is a simple tale, beautifully told, of a wet night at a shepherd's cottage near Casterbridge. Three men knock at the door and ask for shelter. The first is mysterious in that he has, it seems, forgotten his money, his pipe, his tobacco, everything. The second proves to be the hangman on his way to the jail at Casterbridge to hang a sheep-stealer in the morning. The third sees the first two, looks aghast and bolts. We then learn that someone has escaped from Casterbridge jail and the whole company sets off to catch the third stranger whose suspicious behaviour leads them to suppose him the escapee. But the hangman and the first stranger soon tire of this work on a wet night and go their separate ways. When the third stranger is apprehended it turns out that he is not the escapee but his brother and that the escapee, who proves to be the man due to hang on the morrow, was the first stranger who had been drinking and singing with the hangman. This is Hardy's best sort of story, comic, macabre, unexpected, homely, full of rural touches of the finest kind.

'The Withered Arm' is a story of illegitimacy and witchcraft, again involving a hanging and, as usual, taken from the oral traditions of Wessex. 'The Distracted Preacher' is very long for a 'short' story and, apart from a certain briskness of style, seems to have as much of the makings of a novel as *Under the Greenwood Tree*, for instance, in terms of plot, character and structure. Its plot is too long for an adequate *résumé*, but it suffices to say that it involves love as usual and is a historical piece, with something of the flavour of Hardy's novel of the Napoleonic wars, *The Trumpet-Major*, involving smugglers and the exciting life of dwellers on the south coast of England during the century before the novelist's own.

A Changed Man and Other Tales includes several good stories, notably 'The Waiting Supper', 'The Grave by the Handpost' and 'The Romantic Adventures of a Milkmaid'. 'The Waiting Supper' explores yet again the possibilities of love across the great class divisions of Hardy's time. Christine Everard, a 'Lady', promises to marry Nicholas Long, who is not a gentleman. The marriage does not take place, he goes away for fifteen years during which she marries and her husband disappears into 'the bowels of Asia', and is presumed dead, murdered. When Nicholas returns they try once more to get married but Christine's husband sends word that he is alive and is about to return.

The supper she has prepared for Nicholas to celebrate their wedding on the next day is now kept waiting for Christine's long-absent husband. But the husband never comes. Nicholas and Christine wait another seven years (the legal minimum) and he proposes marriage for a third time, but by now they are older (fifty and fifty-three) and, even when the husband's body is finally discovered, they do not think it worth their while to marry. Delay and frustration could hardly be taken further.

'The Grave by the Handpost' is one of the most sombre and affecting of Hardy's stories. It combines, in less than a dozen pages, the comic village choir of the *Under The Greenwood Tree* type, singing on Christmas Eve, and two sadly unnecessary suicides. But it has no love interest and involves no women and, as suicide is rare in Hardy and women common, this in itself makes it an unusual piece for all the familiarity of the musicians and the Napoleonic war setting. The suicides are a father and son, both sergeants in the army at the time of death. The son sends a letter home from India bitterly reproaching his father for having forced him into the army; as a consequence the father shoots himself and is buried in unconsecrated ground, at a crossroads. The son arranges for a reburial in the churchyard but this is never performed and when he returns from the Penninsular Campaign he discovers this and in due course he too shoots himself. Like so many of Hardy's characters, this son suffers from 'super-sensitiveness'; were he a carefree and thoughtless rustic all would perhaps have been well but he is cursed, like Jude Fawley, with a sensitivity that makes his life painful.

'The Romantic Adventures of a Milkmaid' runs to nearly one hundred pages and could perhaps have been expanded into a novel. As it is, however, it receives the brisker treatment of a short story, with less circumstantial detail, in ways that reveal the difference between the two genres: in this story, long as it is, there is no subsidiary plot, no focusing on themes and characters other than the heroine and her lovers. There are no authorial intrusions and we are not invited to share in any of Hardy's philosophical asides, symbolic descriptions or historical meditations; the tale itself is what counts. Margery, a milkmaid, comes upon Baron von Xanten just as he is contemplating suicide and, in gratitude for her intervention, he promises her anything she wants. She chooses to go to a ball with him and, reluctantly, he arranges this. The ball turns her head so that she is no longer interested in her fiancé, Jim, a lime-burner. Jim plays a waiting game and is rewarded when the Baron, thinking himself to be on his death-bed and regretting what he has done to Margery, summons the young couple and more or less forces them to be secretly married there and then. They continue to live apart and the Baron, who seems to love Margery himself, goes abroad. Jim eventually wins his wife for himself by pretending to court another woman and all ends happily, although the Baron does in the end die and Margery appears to have been in his power, almost mesmerised by him.

This story has many of the characteristic motifs of Hardy's fiction, as will be obvious, but the most significant may be the theme of class. Upper-class characters, such as Baron von Xanten, hypnotise people of a lower class. The Baron, with his mysterious origins and his strange name, imbued with the melancholy of a potential suicide and the glamour of great wealth, represents all that a romantic country girl could attribute to her social superiors. He can be seen by the student of Hardy as a symbolic representation of the slightly absurd notions people can have about things of which they are ignorant, in particular the fantastic image of the upper classes that nineteenth-century rustics must have had. Margery sees things at the ball, such as good furniture and candlesticks, that she has never seen before and she yearns desperately for them. She regards the Baron as a fascinating but alien being, almost one of another species. This largely groundless view is all-important for us, a century later, if we are going to try to understand the immense significance of social divisions in Hardy.

All of Hardy's short stories are worth reading, but the student might do best to start with those mentioned in this chapter. As in the case of the 'Milkmaid', it is well worth looking in the stories for evidence of Hardy's main interests and concerns – sometimes they appear there in remarkably sharp focus.

Chapter 8

The poems

STUDENTS OF HARDY who come to his poetry after some initial work on his fiction, hoping for insights that will help them to understand the novels, will not be disappointed. Hardy's poems circle in an ever-changing pattern round a number of well-organised motifs and topics, and they are the same motifs and topics, on the whole, that we have discovered in our discussion of his fiction. As a first example we can taken an early poem, 'Postponement', dated 1866; it is not Hardy's best or greatest piece of verse, but it is highly characteristic of his lyrical output.

Snow-bound in woodland, a mournful word,
Dropt now and then from the bill of a bird,
Reached me on wind-wafts; and thus I heard,
    Wearily waiting: –

'I planned her a nest in a leafless tree;
But the passers eyed and twitted me,
And said: 'How reckless a bird is he,
    Cheerily mating!' '

'Fear-filled, I stayed me till summer-tide,
In lewth of leaves to throne her bride;
But alas! Her love for me waned and died,
    Wearily waiting.'

'Ah, had I been like some I see,
Born to an evergreen nesting-tree,
None had eyed and twitted me,
    Cheerily mating!'

Closely considered, this poem proclaims itself loudly to be by Hardy. It is about love and marriage, it rests in part on the tension between imagined delight, 'Cheerily mating!', and the dreary reality of 'Wearily waiting' that reminds us of all the lovers in Hardy's novels and stories who hope and wait: Gabriel Oak waiting patiently for Bathsheba Everdene in *Far From the Madding Crowd*, Eustacia Vye waiting to be 'loved to madness' in *The Return of the Native*, Lady Constantine waiting for her young astronomer in *Two on a Tower*, Nicholas Long waiting his whole life through for the girl he was betrothed to when only he had remembered it. There is sometimes a tendency to believe that such remarkable statements as these about the government of the universe do not constitute a 'philosophy' and cannot be found expounded in a consistent form anywhere in Hardy's work. But there does seem to be a clear gain in allowing his verse and his prose to mesh together. An identifiable view of the universe does then emerge, and it is the evolutionary one we discussed in Chapter 2: *Something* keeps the universe going (the 'Immanent Will', Hardy called it) but it is a blind and indifferent force, nothing like the God of religions such as Judaism, Christianity or Islam. Pity is man's prerogative and it acts as a deep motivation throughout Hardy's work.

Hardy illustrated his 'philosophy' again and again in his verse. In the sonnet 'Hap' he stresses the indifference of the universe, as we saw in the discussion of this poem in Chapter 1. At the other end of the scale in length we can consider *The Dynasts*, Hardy's largest work and itself a massive illustration of the workings of the 'Immanent Will'.

The Dynasts occupied Hardy for most of the first eight years of the twentieth century and was the result of a lifetime of reading about the Napoleonic wars which had, of course, also formed the background to *The Trumpet-Major*. The 'Epic-Drama', as Hardy called it, covers the ten years that culminated in the Battle of Waterloo (1815). Its intention is to reveal the workings of the world from the perspective of the gods: it opens and closes with scenes set in the 'Overworld' where 'Phantom Intelligences' such as the 'Chorus of the Pities' and the 'Spirit of the Years' discuss the events taking place on the earth below. These spirits also appear from time to time during the drama to comment on the crucial scenes.

The Dynasts strains the resources of the literary medium to breaking-point and it has been suggested that what Hardy was really writing for was the as-yet-uninvented cinema. Only in a film could the transitions between the imaginary world and the real world be made convincingly, and only film could cover the immense scale of the work. Some of the 'stage-directions', in particular, seem written expressly for the cinema, such as this one from Part 1, Act 1, Scene 1:

A stage-coach enters, with passengers outside. Their voices after the foregoing [that is, after the voices of the 'Overworld' of spirits] sound small and commonplace, as from another medium.

There is, of course, a tradition of poets writing plays intended principally for armchair reading ('closet drama'), to be read rather than performed; Shelley's (1792-1822) *The Cenci* (1819) is an example. And even a man of the theatre such as Henrik Ibsen (1828-1906) wrote a number of pieces that are difficult to perform, and are intended to be read, such as *Brand* (1866) and *Peer Gynt* (1867). Conversely there were some attempts to stage *The Dynasts* in the early years after its publication. These, which were necessarily only partial performances, were supplanted by a number of BBC radio adaptations which were broadcast in 1933, 1943, and 1951 and 1967. By all accounts these were successful and worked well in the medium of radio.

Although *The Dynasts* is long, and readers fear they may be puzzled by what exactly it is they are reading, it need not present too much difficulty to the student of Hardy; it may be a larger picture, but it is a well-ordered one that shows Hardy's view of man's relationship with the universe clearly and explicitly. The student of Hardy who is unable, due to pressures of time, to read the work in its entirety would be well advised to read the 'Fore Scene' and the 'After Scene' at least.

The latter, particularly, summarises Hardy's 'philosophy' and his attitude of compassionate doubt. The 'Spirit of the Years' opens the 'After Scene' with the words:

'Thus doth the Great Foresightless mechanize
In blank entrancement now as evermore
Its ceaseless artistries in Circumstance
Of curious stuff and braid, as just forthshown.
    Yet but one flimsy riband of Its web
Have we here watched in weaving-web Enorm . . . '

The 'Spirit of the Years' here describes the 'Immanent Will', the unconscious force that drives the universe, the God asleep who propels the whole machine, weaves the great web. The 'Spirit of the Pities' argues from an evolutionary standpoint that this God may wake up just as man achieved consciousness:

'Thou arguest still the Inadvertent Mind. –
But, even so, shall blankness be for aye?
Men gained cognition with the flux of time,
And wherefore not the Force informing them?'

The 'Spirit of the Pities' cherishes a hope that things will one day be as religious believers think they already are. He introduces a hymn, sung by the 'Pities', saying to the more sceptical 'Spirit of the Years':

'The Will that fed my hope was far from thine,
One I would thus have hymned eternally: – '

The hymn itself involves a fairly orthodox Judaeo-Christian theology, but we remember the 'would' of these introductory lines; even the 'Pities' are agnostics.

The dialogue continues, with the 'Spirit of the Years' sounding very like Hardy himself; affected by the hymn he says:

'You almost charm my long philosophy
Out of my strong-built thought, and bear me back
To when I thanksgave thus . . .
Yea, I psalmed thus and thus . . . but not so now!'

Life for Hardy was loss, and lost faith one of its most painful aspects. He ends by giving the 'Years' his intellectual approbation (the 'All-mover' is unconscious, its processes 'heaving dumbly') but in a joint 'chorus' of both 'Pities' and 'Years', although the former cannot win the argument about the present, the hope is expressed that perhaps the Immanent Will will one day awake:

A thrilling stirs the air
Like to sounds of joyance there
That the rages
Of the ages
Shall be cancelled, and deliverance offered from the darts that were,
Consciousness the Will informing, till It fashion all things fair!

The Dynasts employs some thirty different rhyme-schemes, blank verse and prose, and we can return to Hardy's lyric poetry by way of this hint as to his enormous versatility as a poet. It has been said that, in nearly nine hundred and fifty printed poems, Hardy does not repeat a stanza and rhyme scheme even once. This may not be quite strictly accurate (the sonnets 'Revulsion' and 'She, to Him, 1' seem identical in these respects, for instance) but it is true enough to make us pause and wonder at Hardy's command of the rhythms and possibilities of the English language.

His voice is intensely personal and, as it were, unfashionable. Although he varies stanza form and rhyme scheme with such extraordinary self-assurance, he does not experiment with 'Modernist' techniques, complex metaphors or opaque convolutions. On the other hand he is not noticeably Victorian, either; he does not have the smooth flow of Tennyson or the eccentric dramatic voice of Browning. From the first poems published (the earliest dated are from 1866, though of course they did not see the light of day until 1898) to the last (published posthumously in 1928) Hardy remains unaffectedly and unfashionably his own man. This can sometimes be disconcerting, as for instance when he muses with almost excessive simplicity on some aspect of his own life. 'He Wonders About Himself', for instance, seems almost too slight to be preserved. But more usually this simplicity is devastatingly effective, as for instance in the poem 'The Walk' with its disturbing last line:

You did not walk with me
Of late to the hill-top tree

By the gated ways,
As in earlier days;
You were weak and lame,
So you never came,
And I went alone, and I did not mind,
Not thinking of you as left behind.

I walked up there today
Just in the former way;
Surveyed around
The familiar ground
By myself again:
What difference, then?
Only that underlying sense
Of the look of a room on returning thence.

This is Hardy at his most typical. The stanzas are carefully constructed, the indentations of the lines seem to echo the movements of thought in the poet's mind. The language (vocabulary and syntax) is pared down so much that without rhythm and rhyme this could almost be the mundane prose of a personal letter; so stanza form and rhyme scheme, together with rhythm, *make* the poem – it is not done by metaphor, by complexities of grammar and word-order, by alliteration and assonance, or by rhetorical power. And this means that it is lucid, that we are likely to be convinced that we are looking into the poet's heart, that this is true feeling being expressed. To return for a moment to matters discussed in Chapter 1, a poem like this, being so personal, has to depend on an understanding of the circumstances of its composition. Perhaps this approach involves the reader in the Intentional Fallacy (an attribution of meaning to a literary work, which may be false), but if so then it seems that sometimes such breaking of literary laws is unavoidable. Certainly, if a reader did *not* know the background to this and the other 'Poems 1912-1913' which largely concern the death of Hardy's first wife, Emma, in 1912, he or she would be needlessly cut off from a whole level of sympathy and understanding. Thus, in this poem, it is the age and infirmity of Emma that is hinted at in the word 'lame', and the considerable length of their marriage (almost forty years) that lends pathos to the poet's loneliness; above all, it is Emma's recent death that holds the key to the poem. It is legitimate to ask whether this event, not really revealed in the poem at all, would be apparent to the reader who knew nothing whatever about the author. Biography must be used with care, but it could be excessive purism to exclude it altogether in a case such as this.

'Poems 1912-1913' constitutes the collection widely regarded as Hardy's greatest poetry, and no student of Hardy should remain ignorant of such poems as 'The Voice', 'Beeny Cliff', 'At Castle Boterel' and 'After a Journey'. Besides these, and the other poems we have mentioned, the student could greatly improve his or her general understanding of the author by reading a good number of the poems, more or less at random, and making brief notes about their concerns, motifs, techniques and connexions with the fiction. Patterns will begin to emerge and a more confident view of Hardy's work as a whole will be the result.

As an example, here is a list of some of the poems that might strike a reader of Hardy's first published collection, *Wessex Poems* (1898), together with examples of the kind of notes that a student of Hardy might be likely to make on them.

'Hap': we have discussed this poem: see Chapter 1. Hardy's 'philosophy' in fourteen lines?

'At a Bridal': written in 1866. Hardy has already taken in some of the central points of Darwinism, but here he adds that although 'Love' may 'design' certain 'sovereign types' of humanity, nature is not interested in such fancies.

'Neutral Tones': we begin to feel a strong sense of gloom in this volume of verse. Have human relationships and the universe ever seemed gloomier than to the writer of this poem? What is the view of human relationships we find in the novels?

'Revulsion': 1866 again. How this young man suffers, and how he turns to the old false remedy of sour grapes! As with 'Hap', there is a marvellous balance between the octave and the sextet in this sonnet.

'A Sign-Seeker': there is no evidence of *transcendence* in Hardy's universe. There is nothing *other* than the universe available to man. 'When a man falls, he lies.'

'The Ivy-Wife': survival of the fittest demonstrated in a wood. We think of *The Woodlanders* and also notice Hardy's easy assimilation of trees with men and women.

'A Meeting with Despair': compare the first chapter of *The Return of the Native* with this poem about a man on a moor.

'Friends Beyond': the dead do not and cannot care. So many of these *Wessex Poems* are about death and disappointment, and yet this one, for all its gloom, is written in a beautifully mellifluous and resigned style.

'Thoughts of Phena': Tryphena Sparks? Hardy did not forget his early loves and there is a sense of suppressed emotion here, and of regret, that is echoed in the frustrations of, for example, Giles Winterborne in *The Woodlanders*.

'In a Wood': subtitled 'see *The Woodlanders*'. The poet finds that woods do not offer him the 'sylvan peace' he expected but rather share with men the struggle for survival: they are 'combatants all!'

Indeed, when he turns back to mankind he at least rediscovers that men can smile and talk and, sometimes, can be true to one another. As usual in Hardy, it is in man, not in nature or in God, that a little hope is to be found.

'Nature's Questioning': here Hardy considers nature only, nature without man and, consistently, he finds no hope. The universe seems to be a vast and meaningless machine and although the poet claims that he cannot judge whether this is a true picture ('No answerer I . . .') this is only a technicality, a little nod to agnosticism in the midst of a powerfully atheistic poem.

'The Impercipient': this clinches the point. Here the poet looks not at nature but at man and, although the believers are his 'brethren', he simply cannot see what they see – he can only see indifferent nature. He would *prefer* to believe, but he cannot.

'The Bride-Night Fire': for all his gloom, Hardy can sing us a vigorous ballad. It is, of course, a ballad about strange doings concerning love and marriage. The fire in question has some affinity with the fire in *Desperate Remedies*.

'Heiress and Architect': the fantasy of the young architect given unlimited power by, and here over, a rich young lady. The 'plot' of the poem is reminiscent of *A Laodicean* but the ending adds Hardy's charnel-house touch.

'I look Into My Glass': the last poem in the volume is another of those brief and intense flashes of self-revelation in the style of 'He Wonders About Himself'. It is a strong piece, very simply constructed, and perhaps it offers a model for understanding Hardy's use of imagery. The metaphor is so close to being literal as almost to confuse us when we try to analyse it. 'Wasting skin' is literal; the 'shrinking' of the poet's heart may be partly literal, too, as his body contracts with age; the 'hearts grown cold' could literally be those of the dead as well as metaphorically those of the living but indifferent; 'endless rest' sounds literal in a poet for whom life is a harsh race. Only in the last stanza does the imagery begin to establish its independence with the personification of time, but even here the last line, with its 'throbbings' has a literal reference back to the poet's heart. It is perhaps in this sort of lyric that Hardy achieves his greatest intensity and his greatest success.

These notes have been intended as examples of reactions to Hardy's poetry. All his work forms a 'great web' of cross-references and echoes, and perhaps the most valuable work the student of Hardy can undertake is to read more Hardy.

In conclusion we might consider two contrasting poems, from among the best-known in Hardy's *oeuvre*, 'When I set out for Lyonnesse' of

1870 and 'the Darkling Thrush' of 1900. Such an analysis of these two poems may perhaps catch something of the elusive essence of Hardy's poetry.

The general impression given by the two poems is such that one seems to contradict the other. Life and nature are at a very low ebb indeed in 'The Darkling Thrush' while 'When I set out for Lyonnesse' has a romantic, youthful, magical and optimistic tone. In the former poem a desponding and perhaps ageing man (Hardy was sixty in 1900) looks into a wood on a dark evening in the dead of winter and considers how the nineteenth century is now a 'corpse' among the symbols of death that he finds in the landscape. The associations offered are all utterly negative: in the first stanza alone we encounter 'Frost' that is as gray as a ghost, the 'dregs' of winter, the 'weakening eye of day', the 'tangled' undergrowth of the wood, 'broken lyres', mankind as ghosts, and the chilling cold.

In the 'Lyonnesse' poem, although it starts on a cold morning, when 'rime', or frost, is on the branches, we find far more positive associations: starlight, prophets, wizards, magic and 'radiance rare'. As usual, both poems are intensely personal. There is no reason to suppose the 'I' in either case to be anyone other than Hardy. On New Year's Eve 1900 it is he who takes a solitary walk in the frosty evening; we know that Hardy did take such walks and that he was concerned about the fate of birds in bad weather. Back in 1870 it was Hardy himself, of course, who travelled from Dorset to North Cornwall ('Lyonnesse' – a distance, as we are told in the poem, of a hundred miles) and who there met and fell in love with his future wife. Here again the reader should ask himself how much of this Cornish poem would be really comprehensible to someone entirely ignorant of the facts of Hardy's life.

We have thus already somewhat undermined our original contention that the two poems stand in contradiction to one another. They are both dominated by a strongly marked 'I' who appears in emphatic positions, in the first and last lines of each poem for instance. They are both concerned with the effect of the experience they describe on the emotions of this 'I'. And we can go further than this. There is in both cases a direct link between the 'I' (the poet) and the natural scene that has evoked the poem; the 'pathetic fallacy' is at work although it may at first seem hidden. The weather of 'The Darkling Thrush' is clearly representative of the state of the poet's soul; death approaches the year, the century, the thrush and the poet alike. Similarly there is a hint of the 'pathetic fallacy' in the first stanza of the 'Lyonnesse' poem: the poet is in a frozen state when he sets out, but the 'rime ' is freezing branches laden with blossom ('sprays') so he is perhaps ready to be thawed out and to come to life; he is as lonely as a star, brilliant but remote from the warmth of the world, and soon he will be warmed by love.

Both poems employ simple metrical schemes, varying three-stress and four-stress lines in regular patterns, and both depend heavily on their stanza-forms to make their effect. 'The Darkling Thrush' has a measured tone created by heavy end-stopping in the first two stanzas, especially on the even lines; it would be impossible to rush on after 'spectre-gray', or 'eye of day', or 'broken lyres', or 'household fires'. The sombre mood is reflected in this iambic dead march. Then, after two stanzas of this gloom, the pace quickens a little as Hardy tries to eliminate the end-stopping in the four opening lines of each of the two final stanzas, but he is only partially successful. The heavy regularity of the metre, coming after what has gone before, defeats his attempt at a light and joyful tone and the poem ends on a slow last line that makes its own comment on the carollings of the thrush.

'When I set out for Lyonnesse', as befits a poem in which the poet refers to a secret experience which he intends to keep hidden, has an inward-looking arrangement of lines and stanzas. The repetition of the magical name of Lyonnesse, itself requiring some slightly esoteric knowledge to take on its proper meaning, gives a self-absorbed and incantatory tone to the poem. The last two lines recapitulate the first two with the difference that the neutral, or even rather pessimistic, 'hundred miles' have given way to the optimism of the magic in the poet's eyes which is emphasised by an exclamation mark.

Above all, however, the two poems are comparable in terms of the central mystery they consider, and in this respect they can perhaps stand for all of Hardy's more serious verse. He was, self-confessedly, 'impercipient', but there is often a sense in his poems that he is conscious, as it were, of the thing that he is unable to perceive. He starts nostalgically as if something has been lost to him; sometimes this thing is religious faith, sometimes childhood, often love. Thus he is a 'Sign-Seeker', a 'God-Forgotten' alien; he writes from a position 'By the Earth's Corpse' as if in lament for the life that it once enjoyed. Or he remembers, as in 'The Self-Unseeing', a moment in childhood which was blessed to him but which at the time passed unnoticed:

Everything glowed with a gleam;
Yet we were looking away!

Or he ponders such nostalgic episodes in love as are easy to imagine from a simple list of titles: 'The Superseded', 'The To-Be-Forgotten', 'A Broken Appointment', 'Postponement' and 'She at his Funeral'. Or he is able, as a young man, to dwell on the feelings of a deserted woman, as in the 'She, to Him' sonnets; typically, the first two of these open:

'When you shall see me in the toils of Time,
My lauded beauties carried off from me,
My eyes no longer stars as in their prime . . .'

and 'Perhaps, long hence, when I have passed away . . .'.

In other words the young Hardy imagines a woman imagining how, in the distant future, she will feel about what will by then be the distant past. He goes to considerable lengths to create a mood of nostalgia, but this nostalgia should perhaps be thought of as being between inverted commas; it is, paradoxically, a 'nostalgia' for the present. The thing lost has only taken on its special value *now*, in the present when, precisely, it is too late to recapture it. The 'Poems 1912-1913' is a perfect example of this; Hardy's nostalgia for the present, a quickening of his sense of the ultimate desolation of existence.

To return to 'When I set out for Lyonnesse' and 'The Darkling Thrush', we find that these poems offer different versions of this mysterious amalgamation of the past and the present. Both are in the past tense ('When I *set* out . . . The rime *was*', 'I *leant* upon a coppice gate') and both conceal their final meaning from the reader: in one it is a 'magic' and in the other a 'Hope', the former suggesting love and the latter religious possibilities, but that is only what it seemed like at the time; in the present there is only a memory of a possibility.

Suggestions for further reading

Biographies

GITTINGS, ROBERT: *Young Thomas Hardy,* Heinemann Educational, London, 1975 (Penguin Books, Harmondsworth, 1978).

GITTINGS, ROBERT: *The Older Hardy*, Heinemann Educational, London, 1978 (Penguin Books, Harmondsworth, 1980).

HARDY, F.E.: *The Early Life of Thomas Hardy*, Macmillan, London, 1928.

HARDY, F.E.: *The Later Years of Thomas Hardy*, Macmillan, London, 1930.

MILLGATE, MICHAEL: *Thomas Hardy: A Biography*, Oxford University Press, Oxford, 1982.

O'SULLIVAN, TIMOTHY: *Thomas Hardy: An Illustrated Biography*, Macmillan, London, 1975.

Correspondence and notebooks

The Collected Letters of Thomas Hardy, ed. Purdy and Millgate, Oxford University Press, Oxford, Vol. I, 1980; Vol. II, 1980; Vol. III, 1982. Further volumes in preparation.

The Personal Notebooks of Thomas Hardy, ed. Richard H. Taylor, Macmillan, London, 1979.

Bibliography

GERBER, H.E. and W.E. DAVIS (EDS): *Thomas Hardy: An Annotated Bibliography of Writings About Him,* Northern Illinois University Press, De Kalb, Vol. I, 1973; Vol. II, 1983.

JACKSON, ARLENE M.: *Illustration and the Novels of Thomas Hardy,* Macmillan, London, 1982.

LAIRD, J.T.: *The Shaping of Tess of the Durbervilles,* Oxford University Press, Oxford, 1975.

PURDY, R.L.: *Thomas Hardy: A Bibliographical Study,* Oxford University Press, Oxford, 1954.

Criticism

BUTLER, LANCE ST JOHN: *Thomas Hardy,* Cambridge University Press, Cambridge, 1978.

CECIL, DAVID: *Hardy the Novelist,* Constable, London, 1943.

COX, R.G. (ED.): *Thomas Hardy: The Critical Heritage,* Routledge & Kegan Paul, London, 1970.

DRAPER, R.P. (ED.): *Hardy: The Tragic Novels* (Casebook Series), Macmillan, London, 1975.

GREGOR, IAN: *The Great Web,* Faber, London, 1974.

GUERARD, ALBERT J. (ED.): *Hardy: A Collection of Critical Essays* (Twentieth Century Views), Prentice-Hall, Englewood Cliffs, N.J., 1963.

HALLIDAY, F.E.: *Thomas Hardy: His Life and Work,* Adams and Dart, Bath, 1972.

KRAMER, DALE: *Thomas Hardy: The Forms of Tragedy,* Macmillan, London, 1975.

MARSDEN, KENNETH: *The Poems of Thomas Hardy,* Athlone Press, University of London, London, 1969.

MILLGATE, MICHAEL: *Thomas Hardy: His career as a Novelist,* Bodley Head, London, 1971.

PAGE, NORMAN: *Thomas Hardy,* Routledge & Kegan Paul, London, 1977.

PINION, F.B.: *A Hardy Companion,* Macmillan, London, 1968.

PINION, F.B.: *A Commentary on the Poems of Thomas Hardy,* Macmillan, London, 1976.

SOUTHERINGTON, F.R.: *Hardy's Vision of Man,* Chatto & Windus, London, 1971.

STEWART, J.I.M.: *Thomas Hardy,* Allen Lane, London, 1971.

TAYLOR, DENNIS: *Hardy's Poetry,* Columbia University Press, New York, 1981.

WILLIAMS, MERRYN: *Thomas Hardy and Rural England,* Macmillan, London, 1972.

WILLIAMS, MERRYN: *A Preface to Hardy,* Longman, London, 1976.

Index

The author of this Handbook

LANCE ST JOHN BUTLER was educated at Pembroke College, Cambridge. He taught English in Iraq, Algeria and London before working for a year as a banker in Brazil. He was a lecturer in English at King Abdulaziz University, Jeddah, Saudi Arabia (1970-71), then a post-graduate student at the University of East Anglia (1971-72) before becoming a lecturer at the University of Stirling in 1972. He has edited *Thomas Hardy after Fifty Years* (1977) and *Alternative Hardy* (1989), and written *Thomas Hardy* (1978) and *Samuel Beckett and the Meaning of Being* (1984). He is also the author of York Notes on *Joseph Andrews*, *Moll Flanders* and *Sons and Lovers*.